Flower Decoration in European Homes

FLOWER DECORATION IN EUROPEAN HOMES

Published in Great Britain as The Art of Flowers in Europe

by Laurence Buffet-Challié

flower arrangements by
Jacques Bédat

William Morrow & Company, Inc. New York

Translated from the French:
L'ART DES FLEURS EN EUROPE

Published simultaneously in Canada by
George J. McLeod Limited, Toronto

Printed in Switzerland

Library of Congress Catalog Card Number 77-80900

Contents

INTRODUCTION

The modern style of arranging flowers has been greatly influenced by the traditional schools of flower arrangement in Japan. The Japanese are creators of poetically beautiful flower arrangements and are undisputed leaders of this stylized method, but the traditions of European style are old and equally pleasing. There is much historical evidence of the use of flowers in Europe, the wall paintings of Knossos and the Pompeian garlands are two examples. The miniature and religious painters of the fifteenth century often show a naïve, symbolic sheaf of flowers as part of the decoration beside a statue of the Virgin.

The difference between East and West is, that flower designs in Europe are purely decorative, and their function is to adorn the home by adding life and colour to an interior. Japanese arrangements, on the other hand, are the symbolic expressions of a national philosophy, and style of living. It is difficult for a European to appreciate the metaphysical subtleties of Ikebana, but the elegant simplicity and refinement of the Japanese compositions can harmonize well with modern, European interiors.

I think that this is the first book to compare flower arrangements of different countries – Germany, England, France, Italy and Scandinavia, and it is interesting to see the part played by climate, style of living, and artistic influence in the development of this universal but divergent art. Fortunately styles are not yet standardized so that the reader can make his own comparisons.

This book has been planned to give help and confidence to beginners.

The first part is technical. It contains indispensable, practical advice, because the art of creating an arrangement has to be learned. The amateur will develop a sense of style if shape and form are learned thoroughly first. Every arrangement is accompanied by a diagram and a detailed description so that the model may be copied without difficulty. Apart from one or two exceptional and distinguished designs, there are no tricks in composition or structure. The use of elaborate structures or complicated wiring has been avoided as these are best left to the professional. The amateur is only concerned with how to make the best use of the flowers or foliage in a natural state.

The decorative role of flowers is analysed in the chapter headed 'Arrangements in their settings'. Considerable skill is required to make a design show to the best advantage in relation to its surroundings. The flowers chosen for a reception or large modern living room will be very different from those used in a smaller room, or for a less formal occasion.

Decoration of the dining table is governed by precise rules clearly explained in the text and sketches. However, the illustrations chosen show that fantasy and ingenuity can avoid the banality of keeping too strictly to the rules. The last part of the book describes wild flowers gathered from the woods and fields, and includes dried flowers as well. Wild flowers mirror the changing seasons, and the joy of finding a sprig of lily of the valley, a dead branch, or of smelling a bunch of wild plants is part of the excitement of a country walk.

The flower compositions in this book make use of a wide variety of cultivated plants from temperate zones. Exotic plants are scarce, although progress in horticulture, transport and packing ensures that some rare flowers, from Asia, Africa and Australia, can be found in large cities all the year round. Rarity, however, adds nothing in itself, it is the shape of the flower that is more important. Flower shapes can be divided into different groups. There are the tall, long stemmed ones such as delphiniums, foxgloves, lilies and gladioli; those with round heads, like dahlias, peonies, or roses; flowers with cups, tulips, amaryllis, and anemones, or those that are flat like marigolds, arctotis, daisies and pansies. Some have bell shaped flowers hanging singly on their stems, or grouped together in bunches. There are so many variations that it is usually possible to replace one flower with another of similar contour when making an arrangement.

The beginner should start by copying exactly, as this will be excellent practice in style, and skill will soon be acquired. Confidence in how to use the flowers will then make it easier to create something new by changing a flower or a line and so produce a different effect still keeping to the basic rules. The most beautiful design will reflect the character of its maker, and emanate an unexpected sense of poetry and wonder.

This book is dedicated to all who love flowers, growing, arranging or just contemplating, whatever the source of thier pleasure.

Laurence Buffet-Challié

The contributors to this work are among the finest European specialists in flower decoration:

Jacques Bédat is one of the best known flower decorators in Paris. His creative fantasy and imagination are shown in his arrangements for the Rothschilds; the Duchess of Windsor; Messieurs Patino and Marcel Dassault; for Renault and Citroën. He has provided the flower decoration for many of the great occasions in the capital and throughout France. One can describe him as a poet who expresses himself in flowers. His love of nature comes from the mountains and forests of Switzerland, his birthplace. The decorations illustrated here were done expressly for this work, or photographed at receptions in Paris. He has also been responsible for all the technical advice.

Julia Clements is founder of the *Modern School of Flower Arrangement* in London and author of fourteen books on the subject. A member of the Royal Horticultural Society, she is also a judge, and has often been invited to judge major flower competitions in London, Paris, New York, Italy, Australia and New Zealand. She organizes successful courses and conferences, even in Japan itself.

Sheila Macqueen is the author of several books on English Flower Decoration, and has created many flower pieces for the Royal Family. She was the chief decorator and demonstrator for the famous Constance Spry organisation.

Camilla Cagli Malvasia has made a great contribution to Italian flower decoration. Her knowledge of art and refined aesthetic sense inspire her to create lively compositions in which original ideas combine with the traditional reminiscent of the *Quattrocento* and Venetian paintings. She organizes many conferences and demonstrations and is one of the judges of international exhibitions.

George W. Smith is a young and brilliant interpreter of present day tendencies in Flower Decoration in England. He is universally recognised and has judged international competitions both in England and abroad. He is also the author of a book on flowers as part of the decorative scheme.

My thanks are due to all those who have so kindly co-operated in providing illustrations:
The Royal Horticultural Society, London.

The National Association of Flower Arrangement Societies of Great Britain, and particularly Mrs. Ella Forrester, a national demonstrator and judge.
The magazines: *Connaissance des Arts, Elle, House Beautiful, Maison Française, Schöner Wohnen.*
All the collectors and art lovers who have allowed photographs to be taken in their own homes, notably M. Pierre Balmain, M. and Mme Christian Bourgois, M. and Mme Antenor Patino, Baron and Baronne Guy de Rothschild, M. Zannettacci, the antique dealers and decorators Mme Dugrenot, MM. Michel Beurdeley, Charles Boucaud, Alain Demachy, Jacques Kugel, Nicholas Landau, A. Perpitch.
The decorators of *Formes Finlandaises* and *Knoll International,* Paris.
M. Paul Jovet and Mlle Schotsman of the Laboratories of the Natural History Museum, Paris, who have identified certain flowers and plants.

TECHNICAL ADVICE

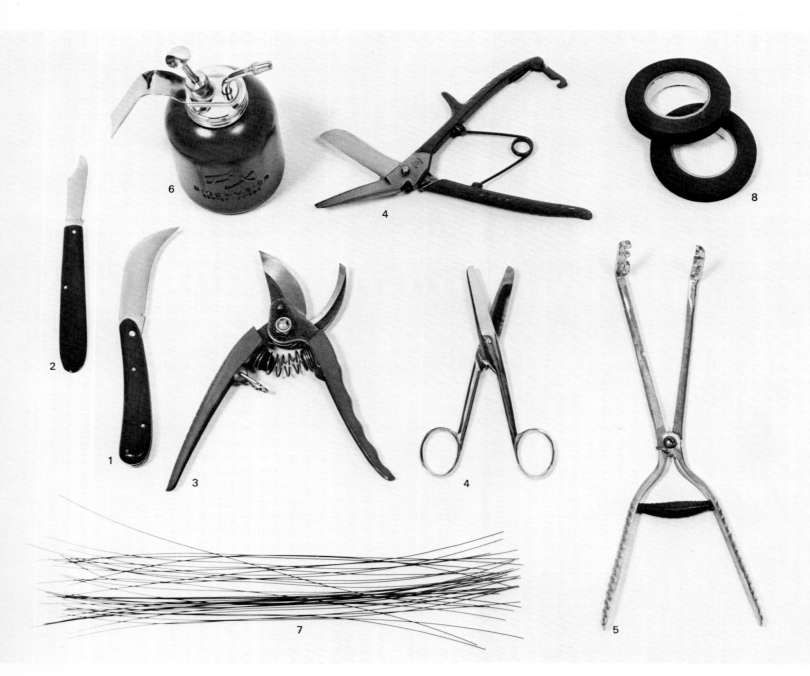

Materials

An inspired work of art cannot be created without suitable tools and materials. A painter or sculptor needs not only colours or stone or wood, but also the tools to work them with. It is the same for the minor art of flower arrangement; certain tools and accessories are necessary; certain rules have to be followed, not only to arrange the flowers, but also to make them last better. The art of creating an arrangement, like all others, calls for technical skill.

Tools
1 A pruning knife for trimming the branches
2 A grafting knife for cutting soft stems, and removing thorns and leaves
3 A pair of secateurs to cut woody stems (roses, lilac, branches of shrubs)
4 A pair of wire cutters or floral scissors for cutting wire, thread, netting, and moss
5 A thorn remover for roses
6 A vaporiser or syringe to refresh the flowers before a reception or in warm weather
7 Florist's wire (sometimes called green wire) to support certain flowers
8 A roll of Floratape
Awls of different sizes, or pointed sticks for making holes in moss to hold soft stemmed flowers.

Flower holders
There is a wide range of flower holders to choose from, and the choice made will depend on the shape of the container, the kind of flowers used, and the style of arrangement to be made.

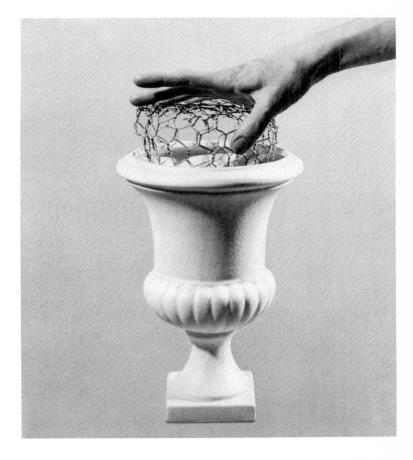

A flower-holder made of wire should be moulded to fit the shape of the vase

Wire netting
Both types of netting are needed; a roll or a piece of the soft type, and some of the slightly stronger kind. The latter will be useful for very large arrangements of heavy flowers. Do not fold or crush this wire into a ball as is often done, but use the

13

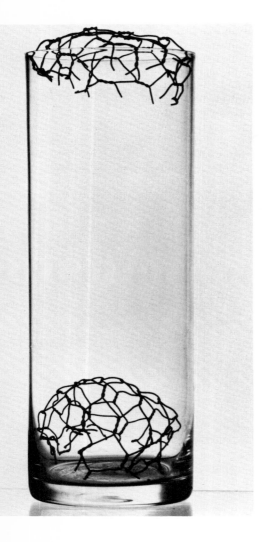

pliers and scissors to make it fit the inside of the vase. For example, in the case of a cylindrical glass vase the netting has to be concealed, and should be cut as follows:

Measure the diameter of the vase and cut a circle of wire of the same size with the floral scissors. Press it into a convex shape, and put it into the bottom of the vase. Cut another round, this time about an inch larger than the neck of the vase. Be sure to cut the netting in the centre of the mesh. Place this netting in the neck of the vase, and turn the edge in all round, hooking the claws of the wire to the wall of the vase.

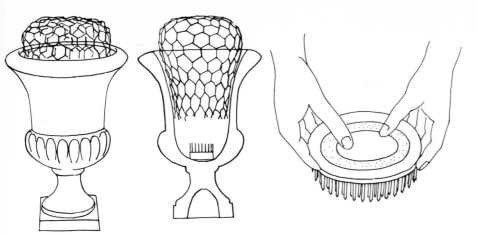

Applying plasticine to the flower-holder so that it fits securely in the vase. Do it before you place it in the water, otherwise it will not stick

Transparent vases of a shape which is not suited to this method should have the netting disguised with green leaves. Be sure to choose leaves which do not rot in water, rhododendron for instance.

Flower holders with points or pinholders (kenzan)
All shapes are available; round, oval, square, rectangular, or some that are made in pairs, and the holders are generally very heavy. The base is metal or lead, and bristles with sharp points. Their weight helps to steady the bottom of a vase, but it is nevertheless advisable to fix them with plasticine. These flower holders are indispensable for modern arrangements made in a low container, using very few flowers after the Japanese style.

For a large arrangement, using heavy flowers, one or more flower holders should be placed at the bottom of the vase, and a grille of wire moulded over the top by pressing it lightly down over the points of the pinholders. A pinch of borax added to the water will prevent rust from forming on metal flower holders.

Mosses
In preference to real moss, which decomposes, use synthetic moss from the florist, or other specialist shops: Oasis, Florapack, Plastimoss, etc. They are sold either in a block or loose. In the piece they look like a light brick, but when full of water they are quite heavy. Part of the block may be cut to the shape of the vase, or several blocks may be piled up, or arranged side by side, depending on the size of the container.

For vases or containers which are not watertight, or for hanging arrangements on walls or beams, wrap a piece of thin plastic round the block to prevent evaporation and leaks.

15

Marbles may be used as flower holders in a transparent glass vase

The loose type of moss should be squeezed in a bowl of water until it is saturated. Then it can be pressed gently into the vase. The plastic moss can be covered with natural moss to improve the appearance.

Agate coloured marbles look attractive in a clear glass vase, and they help to support the flowers, as well as hiding the pinholder.

Various accessories
It is useful to have some stones, pebbles, or gravel of different sizes, both for balance and for disguising the structure.

Containers and supports

Vases

The vase usually determines the style of the arrangement. For example, it is impossible to arrange a modern Japanese composition in a Renaissance vase. Low goblets, narrow flutes, or the ornate vases seen in paintings of the Flemish school are clearly unsuitable for the same reason.

It is therefore useful to own a number of vases, differing in shape, size and material so that any style of arrangement can be made.

Classical arrangements

For these choose simple vases, smooth and of medium height, made of crystal, white or tinted glass; alabaster urns, rectangular or spherical aquariums or tall stemmed glasses. Such vases are useful for arrangements done at the last minute, or to receive flowers brought by guests, until there is time to arrange them properly.

Arrangements in the Period styles

Early period: ewer, altar vase, bronze vessel, pewter goblet or helmet shaped ewer.

18th century: Renaissance vases of cast iron, metal, terracotta, or ceramic; Chinese porcelain vases, Potiches; baluster vases or goblets with slender stems.

Directoire or Empire periods: Goblets on stands, flutes.

Romantic: opaline vases, bowls and goblets.

1900: dark coloured baluster vases; vases in the style of Gallé, and art nouveau; pottery or porcelain in the shape of fish, flowers and so on.

Aquarium vase for spherical arrangements

Modern arrangements

Low arrangements; long, circular, square or rectangular bowls. Tall arrangements; cylindrical or square vases; Scandinavian style lobed vases of all sizes.

Empire flute in engraved glass

Ancient metal ewer

White opaline glass of the Romantic period

Cast iron vase in Renaissance style

Country flowers

Old pewter mugs, jugs, peasant pottery, copper kitchen utensils (saucepans, fishkettles). The choice of container is limited only by one's imagination. Almost anything can be used as a container: old soup tureens, teapots, cups pieces of silver, terra-cotta animals, statues, even boxes by placing a liner inside. A large spiral shell or even a basket, provided it has a metal lining, or synthetic moss wrapped in plastic, makes a very pretty effect. Excess of originality is never a proof of good taste, and substitution can be overdone.

Tray arrangements: usually the tray is entirely covered by the flower arrangement, unless of course it is gold or silver or decorated porcelain.

Arrangement of a single flower: The flower should be a specimen bloom like this magnolia with its circlet of leaves. The vase is black opaline

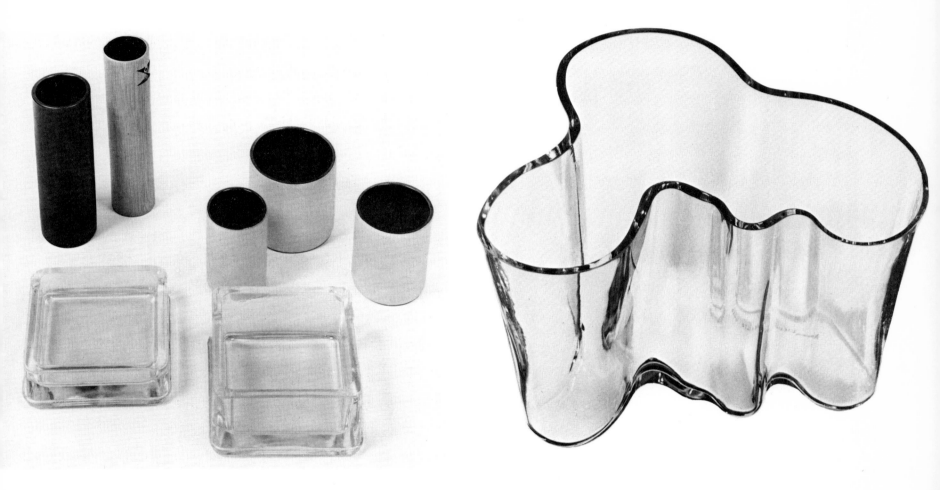

Modern containers: cylindrical vases in different material; glass bowls

Lobed crystal bowl by Alvar Aalto, Finland

A large circular tray of metal or glass or a straight sided basket are useful for low decorations, particularly for table centres. The base is usually covered with damp moss to preserve the flowers during the reception. The edge should be high enough to prevent the water from overflowing.

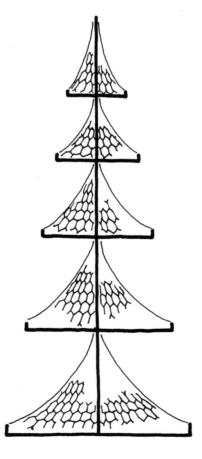

Plain wooden or basket work trays of graded sizes can be used to make a pyramid of flowers, fruit or vegetables. A cone of wire may be fixed to the top tray to give good support to the material and a tall graceful line to the arrangement.

Care of flowers

Flowers, like every other living organism, are fragile. If they are to keep their beauty and freshness for hours or even days they must be handled with special care after they have been cut.

Cutting

The stems should be cut as long as possible. Use secateurs for woody stems, and a grafting knife for soft stems, which should be cut on a slant so that the ducts stay open.

Do not pick in the heat of the day. Flowers should always be cut in the early hours of the morning if they are to stay fresh.

Ignore very young buds or overblown flowers; the first will not open at all, while the latter will drop their petals at the first breath of air.

Cleaning

Pull off the lower leaves, as they rot in the water and smell disagreeable. Remove any faded leaves or bruised petals. Stand the flowers upright in a large bucket filled with water up to two-thirds of their height, and keep in a cool dark place. Leave them until you are ready to use them.

Hot-house flowers should never be suddenly subjected to cold. If they are cut beforehand, they should be stood in water in the hot-house, or kept at the same temperature until they are needed.

Preparation

Before starting the arrangement, cut a little off the end of each stem. It is beneficial to cut the stems under water, and at a slant for soft stemmed flowers. If the stalks are woody they should be split up to an inch or two from the ends to allow the water to be absorbed freely.

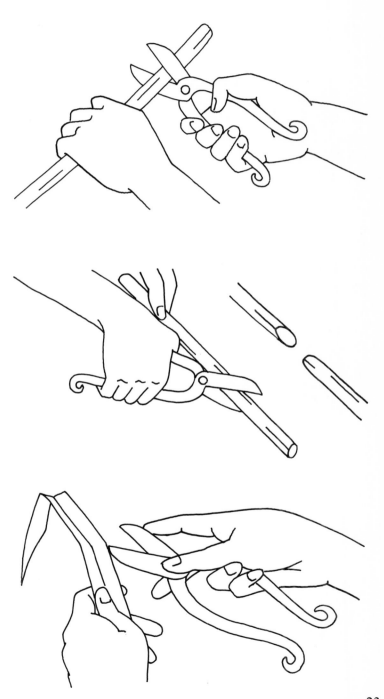

Dip milky stems, such as euphorbia in an inch or two of boiling water. This treatment is also suitable for hollow stemmed flowers like poppies.

To strengthen brittle or hollow stems: slide a piece of wire or a small stick inside. A stem that is too short can be lenthened by inserting it in a straw which will draw up the water by capillary action.

Preservation

A flower that fades before it opens can be revived. Pour some warm water, about 60 degrees, into a bowl. Plunge several inches of the stalk into the water, and cut off an inch, still under water, across the stem. Leave it to soak for several seconds, and then place the flowers upright in a bucket full of cold water. Only the heads must be out of water, and if necessary, should be supported. Leave for an hour.

For faded roses and peonies, proceed as follows: wrap them up completely in newspaper closing the ends, and place them flat in a bath containing just over a inch of water. After a few hours, the flowers will be completely fresh again.

Change the water often, every day if the vase is a small one. Thoroughly clean the container. Add, either three drops of parazone to a quart of water, or an aspirin: both methods prevent the water from polluting too rapidly. Products made for the purpose are also available.

Every time the water is changed, cut off part of the stalk, and remove all dead leaves.

For very large vases that are difficult to handle, take out the flowers and spiked holder together, and plunge them into a bowl of fresh water. Should this prove too difficult, add fresh water daily with some small pieces of ice to counteract evaporation. Avoid putting an arrangement in the sun, or near heat, or in a draught. In warm weather, in a dry atmosphere, or before a reception, spray the flowers with fresh water with a syringe or a vaporiser.

Buying flowers

Plan what flowers you need before buying. If necessary order them in advance, and so avoid disappointment.

Do not choose flowers with black stems, drooping leaves or those that have been wired.

Shape

A flower arrangement is made up of shape, size, and colour. The shape is all important, and the method by which it is achieved must be understood. In many ways a sensitive eye is better than the most elaborate rules and techniques. But inspiration is useless without some basic rules. The success of an arrangement is a question too, of balance, of blending colours, and of the relation between the flowers, the vase, and the intended setting.

Every flower arrangement is contained within a geometrical shape. Even those untidy compositions in paintings by the Great Masters follow this rule. They show that variations of the use of this shape can still preserve the harmony of the whole.

Later, we will study the different possibilities in detail.

Choice of flowers
The first thing is to avoid the conventional, for nothing is more artificial than a choice based on arbitrary rules; the resultant arrangement will look very uninspired. Look closely at flowers growing naturally. Bold contrasts are found everywhere. The tiny violet grows in a forest, and bindweed spreads at the foot of a foxglove. Noticing these contrasts in nature, can suggest ideas for combining the flowers chosen for an arrangement. One thing should be noted, wild flowers do not combine readily with exotic blooms, such as strelitzias or anthuriums. Only those with great experience should attempt this combination, although Jacques Bédat has done so successfully on several occasions.

Flower arrangements in the home
If possible the arrangement should be made in its final position. It is then much easier to make it fit the setting. A tall, imposing composition is only suitable for a large reception

A round bouquet is suitable for a *guéridon* or low table. Seen from above it appears to be in relief

room. There must be plenty of space round such a decoration. In a cramped area it will look constricted and completely spoil the effect.

Never place a tall or spindly arrangement on a heavy piece of furniture, such as a commode, chest, or sideboard; a broader composition is more suitable.

A symmetrical bouquet is always set in the middle of its support (table, mantelpiece, etc.)

An asymmetrical bouquet is set to one side and the balance complemented by a small work of art or painting

Round arrangements to be seen from all sides, should be placed on a stand or table near a sofa, where, with objets d'art it can from the principle element in a decorative composition.

The corner piece to be seen from the front and sides, should be solid, and the front and sides emphasized. It should be tall as it is designed to fill an empty corner.

A symmetrical composition fits perfectly in a classic setting, in the centre of a chimneypiece, a console or a panel. Seen form the front and sides, it resembles the corner arrangement in its sculptural effect.

Asymmetrical arrangement demands a subtle balance. This is the type of modern arrangement pivoting on a line which gives it movement, and is often Oriental in inspiration. If it is placed on a long piece of furniture, or a mantelpiece, it must be set to one side, so as to create a curving line in contrast to the straight line of the support.

Colour

From the earliest records of painting, artists have always painted flowers, delighting in the creation of delicate and brilliant coloured compositions. But the eye of the amateur is untrained. How can he avoid the discordant, dull, or vulgar? To learn to *see* the colours, to create harmonies is no more difficult than learning to read.

Everyone knows that light is broken by a prism into seven primary colours: violet, indigo, blue, green, yellow, orange, red. These colours reflect the light with greater or lesser intensity producing secondary colours.

The diagram shown here allows one to see the transition from one colour to another. On the left, the warm shades: purple, red, orange-red, orange, yellow-orange, yellow. On the right, the cold tones, green-yellow, green, blue-green, blue, blue-violet, violet. Analogous colours are to be found beside each other on the circle, each reflecting its neighbour, (yellow, yellow-orange, for example). Complementary colours are opposite (yellow and violet; red and green, etc.).

Using this diagram it is easy to create a good combination. Flowers in the same colour range serve for decoration in one tone, *en camaïeu;* complementary colours make a bouquet of contrasts.

Naturally, these are only suggestions. The range of colour in flowers is far more varied than that of the diagram, and allows the subtlest combinations, especially of pastel tones.

The room itself determines the colour of the arrangement, either in absolute contrast or repeating several elements in the décor, so that it harmonizes perfectly with its setting.

Monochrome
The monochrome arrangement is in complete contrast to the dominant colour in the background. For instance:

red roses on a white ground, yellow tulips on a background of pale blue, or dark green.

White flowers would be lost in a room where the predominating colour is white. On the other hand against a red or vivid blue background they stand out brilliantly.

However, the subtlety of a delicate white or pastel setting is enhanced by white, as, for instance, white flowers on a white tablecloth in a dining room with painted greyish-white panels or furniture.

Camaïeu (single tones)

The analogous shades of a bouquet *en camaïeu,* produce a rather mysterious and more subtle effect than a monochrome. It is better to aim for harmony rather than contrast with the setting. Shaded blue delphiniums would look magnificent against the bluish-grey and white tones of a Louis XVI interior.

Polychrome

Contrast being principally the territory of single colour arrangements, it is best to harmonize mixed flowers with the principal landmarks in a room, curtains, chair covers, furniture or objects. If the dominant colours – of curtains or a painting for example – are repeated, the result is always effective. It should not be forgotten that a flower decoration has a value of its own; it should therefore not be identical with a wallpaper or the hangings, but should rather accentuate different shades.

The effect of foliage should not be forgotten: it can be used to break a too solid effect, create a curve, when the frame is too rigid, and soften a harsh contrast. It is best to use the natural leaves of the flowers, but sometimes a different foliage can give a better effect.

Mix warm and cold shades freely. Look for good contrast and group together flowers of the same shade, for greater effect, do not scatter them throughout the arrangement.

Bouquets of half-tones are like a misty dream: in a simple glass spherical bowl mix a few bluish agapanthus, pinkish-blue delphiniums, blue scabious, greyish-blue thistles and a tuft of grasses.

Agapanthus, echinops, delphiniums, scabious and grasses. A classic bouquet in shaded tones in a plain glass bowl

BASIC SHAPES

Circle

Round arrangements are meant to be seen from all sides. They need a lot of flowers, packed solidly together. The success of such arrangements depends on the right choice of colours for the flowers, though the use of some contrasting foliage can be attractive.

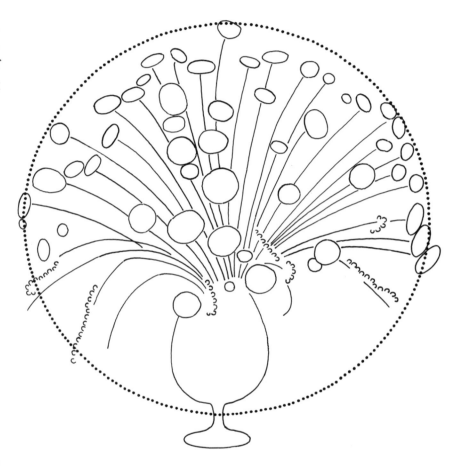

Container
Spherical glass vase

Composition
Korean Chrysanthemums
Euphorbia
Baccara Roses
Pale apricot tulips
Foliage

Method
Put some large gauge wire netting into the mouth of the vase. Then insert several leafy twigs to make a foundation. Arrange the largest flowers (tulips and chrysanthemums) in groups of two or three, so that they make balanced splashes of colour. The stems of these should be long enough to touch criss-cross at the bottom of the vase. This nucleus is then surrounded with more delicate flowers, such as euphorbia, or roses. Use these on long stems: as they are thin they will fill in well without using up too much space. Fill in the empty spaces with shorter flowers. Finally fit in a spike of euphorbia at the base, taking care not to disarrange the flowers near it, and add some small flowers round the rim to hide the netting.

Remarks
This arrangement looks well placed on a table or stand, and is suitable for a formal setting. Here it was made to blend with the warm tones of the room, but the colours used were brighter, and made a strong impact.

Variants
In a different setting the arrangement might look well in paler colours; blue, rose, mauve, or all white, and the line softened by using flowers with more curving stems.

Vertical line

A transparent vase was used for this arrangement. It resembles a pillar, the line being unbroken from top to bottom. It is seen to best advantage either on the ground, or put at the end of a long low piece of furniture. It does not look well when put near other large objects of the same height, as each spoils the effect of the other.

Container
Glass vase shaped like a paralleliped

Composition
Anemones
Forsythia
Iris
Green and pink curly cabbage leaves

Method
The tall branch of forsythia is cut to a length that is roughly three times the height of the vase. It is then put in on the right of the vase. This forms the axis of the arrangement, and the iris and anemones are put round it. The small branch of forsythia on the left makes the arrangement more graceful without spoiling the line. The cabbage leaf on the right helps to balance the central flowers.

Remarks
The stalks must touch the bottom of the vase, and so make a continuous line from top to bottom.

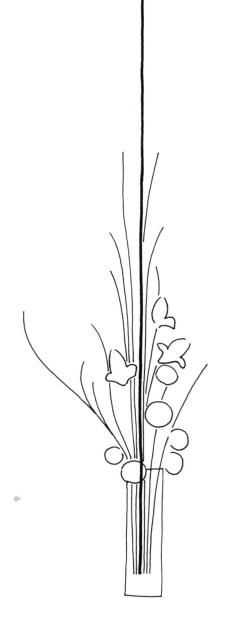

34

Star

The flowers are arranged like stars in a constellation. This clear cut composition looks better against a monochrome background. It could also look well on the shelf of a book-case.

Container
Cylindrical glass vase

Composition
Magnolia
Amaryllis

Method
Choose branches of magnolia with open flowers, and buds, but with very few leaves. Leave the small leaves near the flowers and strip off the rest. A flower holder is not necessary. Place the main branch of magnolia slightly to the left, with its stem touching the bottom of the vase. The other branch with more, smaller flowers is placed to act as a counter balance on the right.

Three amaryllis form a splash of colour at the side, with three caladium leaves behind.

Remarks
This very simple arrangement is cleverly designed. It relies on the balance between the two flowers. Do not overload it with larger flowers; the three shown in the sketch are sufficient, and the elegant branches follow their own natural curves.

Variants
A similar arrangement could be made using sprays of apple blossom.

36

Fan

This is a flat arrangement inspired by the shape of a fan. It is the easiest to make of all the geometrical shapes. The effect is produced by colour contrast; white against bright blue. Suitable for a modern setting, stark furniture and Japanese bric-a-brac. The flowers themselves are of minor interest: it is the overall decorative effect that makes the impact.

Container
Small rectangle of thick glass

Composition
White chrysanthemums

Method
Mould some wire netting to fit the container. Strip off the lower leaves of the flowers and cut the stems. Start at the back, in the centre. Choose the tallest flower and put it in the centre. Then gradually make the spokes of the fan, shortening each stem a little, and keeping in mind the outline shape, the gentle curve of a fan. Keep the stems close to the central one. Fill up the spaces, but do not overcrowd the flowers. There should be plenty of space round such a large arrangement. In this case the leaves help to lighten the massed effect.

Remarks
The basic shape of this arrangement would suit many rooms if a different container were chosen and the colour scheme altered to suit the surroundings.

Variants
Tulips, iris or peonies could be substituted, but they should be of contrasting colours to the background; white/red, yellow/blue, purple/yellow, or orange and light blue.

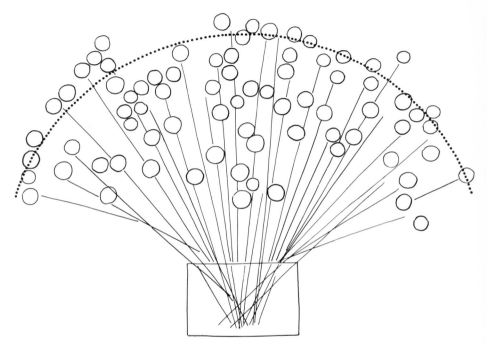

Rectangle

In this arrangement there is no focal point. The flowers are simply placed upright in the vase. Decide on the height required, but do not cut all the stems at first, cut them as you go along. This will make it easier to build up the shape and distribute the colours. This modern design is suitable for many different styles of décor, but it would look better on a commode, sideboard, or console table, rather than a stand or occasional table.

Container
Shallow bowl or oval jardinière

Composition

Agapanthus	Lilac
Anemones	Antirrhinums
Korean chrysanthemums	Narcissi
Gerberas	Roses
Blue iris	Tulips
Daffodils	

Method

Line the inside of the container with synthetic moss. The tall flowers form the line of this design. They are placed at the back of the vase: roses and agapanthus to the right, chrysanthemums to the left. Allow plenty of space between each flower to give lightness to the top. Then put in the flowers in the centre, at the bottom. These are put in vertically, and an open tulip between two gerberas makes a bold focal point. Fill up the remaining spaces with anemones, iris, daffodils and narcissi. The line is softened by a few branches of lilac on the right.

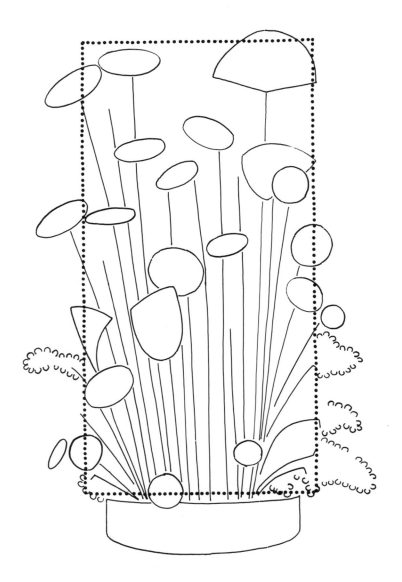

Remarks

Do not group the flowers in clumps, allow enough space between each one. The effect will be heavy if they are too compact.

Equilateral triangle

This is the Classical style at its best, but the shape still suits the twentieth century. It has a number of variations, but the basis is an equilateral or an isosceles triangle. The sides may be elongated, or the triangle placed centrally, or to one side of the vase. Our example is perfectly equilateral. It would be suitable in almost any room as long as the flowers chosen harmonize with the décor. For a blue background Julia Clements chose pale and deep shades of pink with a group of dark mauve roses to stand out against the paler flowers. At the top three bluish-mauve delphiniums rise up like a misty peak, while the flowers at the base curve naturally and seem to move like the branches of a tree.

Container
Traditional urn shaped vase

Composition
Delphiniums
Double stocks
Antirrhinums
Sweet peas
Polyanthus roses

Method

Cut some wire netting and mould it to fit the vase. The three delphiniums are put in the centre, at the back: the longest should measure about one and a half times the height of the vase. Then place two of the stems of stocks on either side: these must be of equal length, and put in slanting they form the base of the triangle. The roses are the focal point of the arrangement, and are grouped together in the centre, with some overlapping the rim of the vase. Fill in the remaining flowers without spoiling the outline shape: all the flowers should radiate from the same point (as shown in the diagram).

Remarks
This arrangement is quite suitable for use on a pedestal, but it can look a little heavy. If a few blooms are loosened in the front it will lighten the effect, and show to better advantage from the sides.

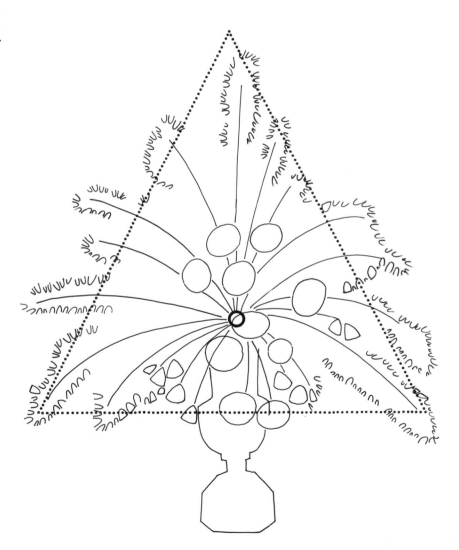

Equilateral triangle (variation)

The composition here is nearly horizontal, but the bottom line is low and curving, and the colours soft: blue, mauve, pink; they give a restful effect. This arrangement should be seen from the front at eye level.

The movement is symmetrical, and develops outwards. Never lose this line or the effect will be spoilt.

Container
A carved candlestick, surmounted by a bowl

Composition

Alstroemeria	Freesias
Cattleyas	Orchids
Cedrus Atlantica glauca	Sweet peas

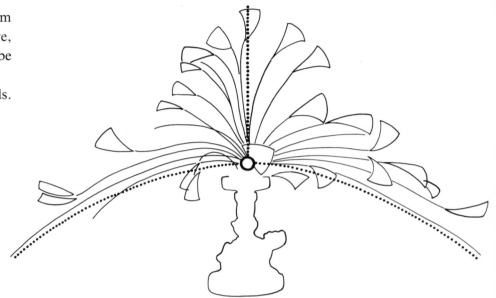

Method
Place a spiked flower holder into the bowl and put over it a small piece of netting, pressing it down until the spikes grip the mesh firmly.

Choose two equal branches of blue Cedrus Atlantica glauca. They should be one and a half times the height of the vase, and be placed horizontally in the vase. At the same time bend the branches twenty-five degrees below the horizontal so as to maintain symmetry. Disguise the flower holder with leaves and small branches stuck through the wire.

The tallest flowers in the centre are cut to a height equal to that of the vase. These are then put in at the back. The structure of the design is now ready; filling in is all that is left. Do not break the symmetrical, curving line and always start from the same point at the bottom.

Pliant stemmed flowers are arranged sideways in the axis of the cedar, never going below its lower line, which should resemble a clean brushstroke.

The sweet peas should be grouped in the middle. Bring to the foreground a small branch and several blooms to give the composition depth.

Remarks
Although this is largely seen from the front, the sides should be as tidy as possible.

Variants
Unlimited possibilities:
In the spring: forsythia, tulips, narcissi
In summer: roses, gladioli, campanula
In the autumn: leaves, dahlias, chrysanthemums.

Asymmetrical triangle

In order to preserve the asymmetrical effect, the flowers are placed slightly to the left of the vase, while those on the right taper sharply. This is a Western adaptation of certain rules of Japanese flower decoration.

Container
Statuette surmounted by a goblet

Composition
Korean chrysanthemums
Plantains
Lilies
Carnations
Oak leaves

Method
Fill the goblet with Oasis moss, so that it is higher than the rim. If necessary fix it with a piece of wire netting.

Start the outline of the arrangement with two oak branches, placing the tallest at the back and to the left. They should be one and a half times the height of the vase. Then put the other branch in front near the bottom.

Some of the flowers – lilies, carnations and chrysanthemums should be arranged at the axis of these oak branches.

Finish the arrangement with long stalked flowers, which will fill out the design without breaking the asymmetrical line. Accentuate the line with a few spikes of plantain.

Remarks
The arrangement shown here is characteristic of this shape but it is suitable for many different sorts of container; a bowl, a pedestal glass, a low bowl, or a simple tray on a pedestal, without altering the basic design.

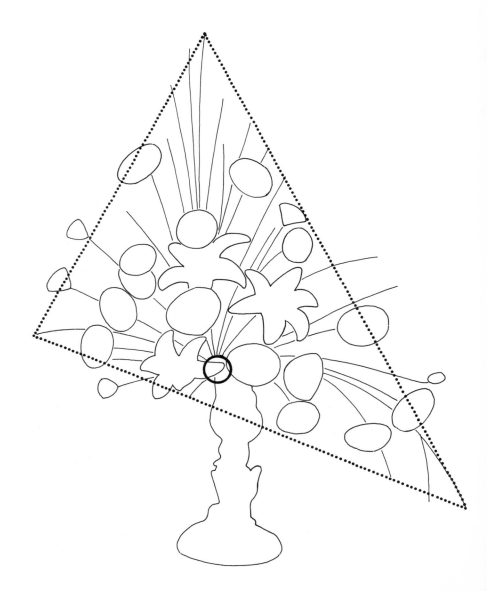

Spheres

At first sight nothing looks easier than to make a spherical bouquet. The flowers are simple, of the same length, the shape, round and solid. In fact, it can be made in a number of ways. Here we illustrate three: one each from Germany, the United States and France. They show the different effects created by varying the kind of flowers used.

 Flowers with a cup (tulips, daffodils, freesias)
 Open flowers (dahlias, carnations, roses)
 Flat flowers 'with faces' (anemones, daisies)

The German version uses flowers with a cup making them stand out in relief. Like the god Janus, this composition has two faces: one pale, made of white and pale yellow flowers, the other a mass of brilliant flowers.

Container
A low pedestal glass chosen to lighten the solid effect

Composition
Freesias
Daffodils
Tulips

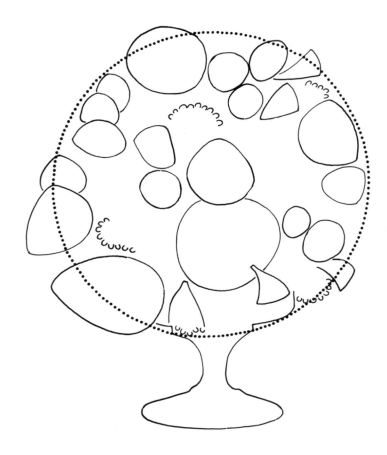

Method

Fill the vase with synthetic moss shaped like a ball. Do not squeeze it too hard; it needs to be firm so that soft stems can be put in smoothly. If necessary, make some holes first with a pointed stick; insert a thin stick to strengthen hollow stems.

 Cover the moss with wire and carpet the surface with greenery. Start the arrangement with the pale flowers, tulips, daffodils and white freesias on one side, and the bright colours on the other side.

All the stems must converge towards a focal point in the middle of the goblet. Uniform distribution of one type of flower makes the arrangement look monotonous. Break up the compact shape of the tulips by using a few daffodils and freesias. The foliage used here is only a background, but it enhances the brilliance of the flowers.

Remarks

As it is very close-knit at the top and centre, the arrangement should be lightened at the base. Loosen a few of the flowers round the edge.

Spheres

Two different faces of the 'Janus' bouquet: *Left:* Front view, monochrome, white tulips and daffodils. *Right:* Reverse, polychrome, anemones, freesias, hyacinths, daffodils and red tulips

Container
Ceramic bowl decorated in the style of 18th-century Chelsea porcelain

Composition
Flame coloured decorative dahlias and crimson pom-pom dahlias

Method
Cut some netting and fit it into the vase. First, put in the dahlias round the edge.

Continue adding flowers towards the centre. Do not cut all the stems to an even height; some of the flowers should appear to be inset, and give an impression of depth. Finish the top with a bud or a thin piece of foliage.

Remarks
With rather heavy flowers, such as dahlias, the size of the arrangement should be at least twice that of the vase. Do not use the giant blooms, they are not suitable for this design.

Prepare the anemones. Cut the stalks straight and arrange a piece of wire netting at the bottom of the container (a glass bowl).

Continue adding flowers closely towards the centre. Grade the height of the flower heads gradually and as the circle shrinks, the flowers will stand more upright.

Start with the flowers round the edge of the bowl. Intertwine the stems between the wires so as to give a firm hold.

The arrangement when finished is round and solid but the shape of the flowers relieves the heaviness.

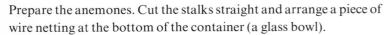

The Hogarth Line

The great 18th-century English painter William Hogarth sometimes drew a small palette beside his signature with an incurving line, and the words, 'the line of beauty'. Curving and sinuous, the so-called 'Hogarth Line' has had some influence on flower decoration in England.

It is not an arrangement for beginners as it demands experience and a sure eye to attain its balanced proportions.

Container
Figure of a girl. This rather tall foundation allows free play of the Hogarth Line

Composition

Astilbe	Red carnations
Begonia Rex	Red roses
Genista (broom)	

Method
The figure is surmounted by a rather deep bowl containing a rounded block of synthetic moss. This should be surrounded with wire netting to anchor it firmly to the base; the stability of the arrangement depends on the flower holder.

Select some of the broom: the principal branch should measure about one and a half times the height of the figure. Cut the other branches in diminishing lengths. Place the upright branch in the centre, slightly towards the back, and another one in front curving downwards. The shorter branches of broom spring from the axis of these two main branches.
Astilbe, begonia leaves, carnations and roses are grouped in the centre. As one fills in, the flowers with longer stalks must be put in first working from the top to the low curved ones alternately, following the original line.

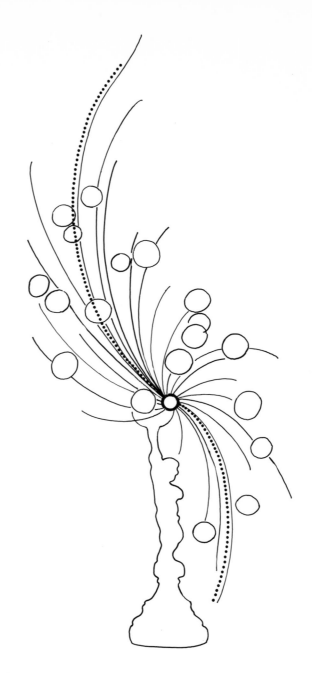

Variants
All types of pliant shrubs may be used for this type of arrangement. Depending on the season replace the roses and carnations with daffodils, tulips, dahlias, chrysanthemums, lilies. Always choose open flowers for the central part of the design.

The diagonal

The principle is the same as in the *Hogarth Line* (preceding page): one group of flowers directed upwards, and another downwards. But the line is not so curved. It is so graceful that it appears to be fluid, flowing diagonally across the figure, almost defying the laws of balance.

Container
Statue of a woman with raised arms, bearing a goblet

Composition

Funkia	Roses
Carnations	Alstroemeria
Antirrhinums	

Foliage: Eucalyptus, grevillea robusta, wild roses

Method
Put a block of Oasis moss into the goblet, coming well above the edge. Reinforce it with a piece of wire netting with a large mesh. In the centre place one or two branches of eucalyptus leaning slightly backwards to mark the tall line of the arrangement. Add a branch of wild rose, bending downwards

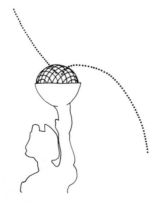

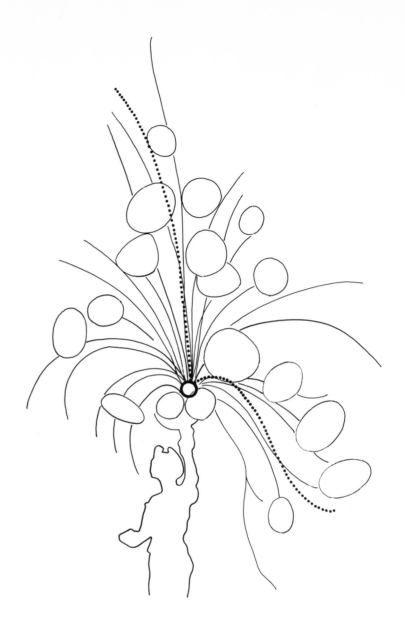

and almost perpendicular to the figure. It is essential that the two branches form a continuous, supple, diagonal line. Finish the arrangement with the remaining flowers following this vertical shape.

Remarks
The large, open flowers are not grouped at the focal point, but follow the oblique line of the arrangement.

PERIOD ARRANGEMENTS

Early Period

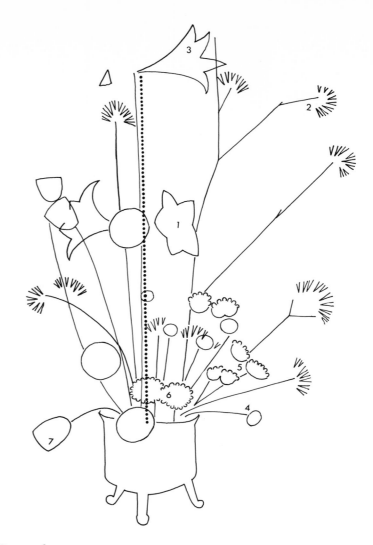

In the middle ages, flowers were largely cultivated for medicinal purposes or to decorate churches. The first arrangements appear in the 15th century, in miniatures or religious pictures; a simple sheaf of flowers beside a figure of the Virgin. These flowers were symbolical and were often shown with other medicinal herbs which were cultivated in cloistered gardens. This arrangement makes no claim to be a reproduction: the amaryllis was unknown in Europe, and the tulip, an oriental flower, was only imported in 1560. However, it is inspired by the flower paintings of the period.

Container
Small bronze tripod of early style

Composition

Amaryllis (1)	Sweet William (5)
Wild parsley (2)	Wild mignonette (6)
Lilies (3)	Tulips (7)
Pinks (4)	

Method
Put a flower holder (pinholder or wire) in the vase. Place the white lilies and the amaryllis in the centre, slightly towards the back (the amaryllis should be about halfway between the vase and the head of the lily). On the left of the rim three tulips lean forward, while two more, rather longer, rise straight up above them. The airy stalks of wild parsley on the right balance the composition. The bottom is filled in with pinks and wild mignonette.

Remarks
This bouquet would be suitable for a Louis XIII, or country interior. In our illustration it stands out in relief against fine oak panelling.

Variants
Instead of wild parsley, use grass and corn. Replace the tulips with thistles, the pinks with berries, daisies and scabious. There should always be some white flowers, so in place of the lily, use garden roses.

A fritillary or Crown Imperial strikes exactly the right note in this arrangement.

Renaissance

The tall line of this composition is determined by the vase. It is a simplified variation of the preceding arrangement and is reminiscent of the flowers decorating the religious and mythological paintings of the early 16th century. Resemblance does not imply a copy; it would be useless to try to imitate a painter's work. His surroundings, the light, and the inspiration of the artist as he worked can never be recaptured.

Container
A pewter altar-vase of the 16th century

Composition

Amaryllis	Wild mignonette
Wild parsley	Gypsophila
White lily	Tulip

Method
Place the long branch of wild parsley upright in the vase. It should be twice the height of the vase.

The amaryllis – the only solid part of the composition – is placed in the centre between the rim of the vase and the top of the parsley.

The large white lily, projecting on the left, is cut short. Put in the dark purple tulip so that it stands in line with the amaryllis but lower. Add the gypsophila and mignonette lower down, but they must not obscure the elegant handles of the vase.

Remarks
The arrangement shows up well against natural oak panelling of the 17th century.

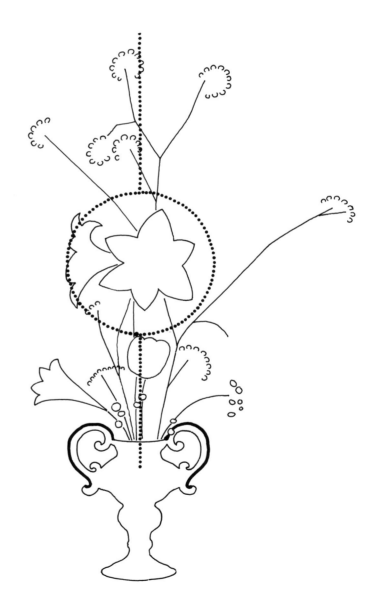

62

Louis XIV

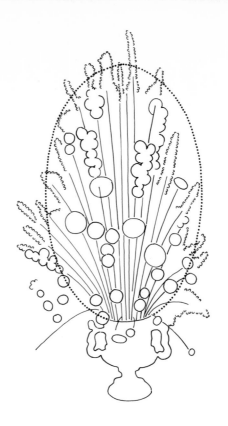

Large, formal and sumptuous, this decoration suits the ostentatious style of the period. The heavy, oval shape gives a massed effect reminiscent of the Dutch flower paintings of the same period.

This lavish decoration is suitable for a large and splendid reception room. Jacques Bédat has used only brilliantly coloured garden flowers in the traditional manner.

Container
A silver-gilt urn; German 17th century

Composition

Nasturtiums	Antirrhinums
Wild clematis	Magnolia
Cosmea	Poppies
Coreopsis	Phlox
Helenium	Polygonum
Delphiniums	Garden roses in clusters
Godetia	Hollyhock
Lavatera	Annual scabious
Tiger lilies	Zinnias
Lupins	

Method
Be sure to fix the arrangement firmly from the beginning because the flowers are heavy. At the bottom of the vase place one or more pinholders and over them some large meshed wire netting. Put the hollyhocks in the middle; they are tall and straight and form the axis of the bouquet. Arrange the rest of the flowers to each side graded in height. Always start from the back. As a rule long flowers, such as delphiniums, lupins, and antirrhinums form the outline.

Fill in the centre of the arrangement. Contrary to the usual rules, the large, round heads are high up, the smaller ones fall over the edge of the vase. The outline should not look rigid; a few single flowers should stand out. At the bottom a magnolia bud seems to peer mysteriously from a dark cave, and nasturtium entwines the sculptured handle. A branch of wild clematis falls towards the foot. The basic solidity of this arrangement does not exclude some lightness, and this adds vivacity without destroying the line.

Remarks
To be successful this bouquet needs garden flowers. Exotic blooms would spoil the effect of natural, fresh abundance.

Variants
White lilies, red and yellow roses, peonies, pink, red or white phlox, grasses, and a few branches of philadelphus.

Louis XV

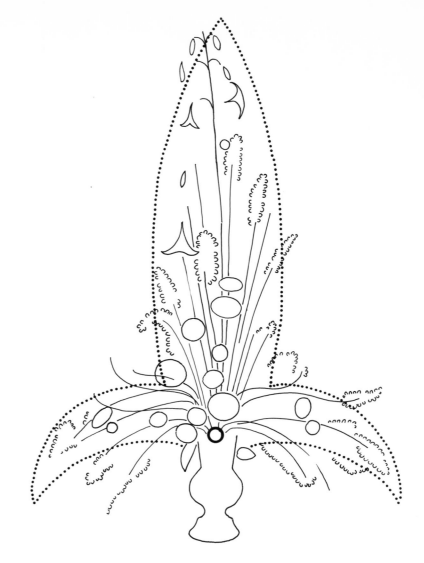

At this period the art of decoration changed, abandoning the heavy outlines of the preceding style and giving place to a finer, curving line. This composition is mid-eighteenth century in inspiration. The outline looks like a fountain, rising and falling. Now the shape is lighter than before, but it is balanced and symmetrical. The flowers all come from the garden, and fresh, light colours are used.

Container
Baluster-shaped copper vase of the 18th century

Composition

Cosmea	Lupins
Coreopsis	Antirrhinums
Delphiniums	Sage
Gaillardia	Statice
Helenium	Scabious
Ivy	Zinnias
Tiger lilies	

Method
The vase is deep enough to dispense with a flower holder. Put a tiger lily and several delphiniums firmly into the vase. The height should be about twice that of the vase, not including the length of the stems inside.

Outline the shape at the base with the most pliant stems of delphiniums, lupins, nasturtiums. Work always from the centre.

Complete the arrangement, but do not break the shape. Tall flowers form the line while those with 'faces', cosmea, coreopsis, scabious and zinnias, form the mass. Group the large flower-heads in the centre and near the bottom.

Several small flowers should jut out round the edge: sage and gaillardias. Place a slanting branch of ivy in the front,

and two or three slender lupins. It should not be absolutely symmetrical.

Remarks
The elegance of this arrangement depends on its proportions: the height is greater than the width of the base by one third.

Variants
A very beautiful decorative effect may be obtained with various coloured antirrhinums, white, red and salmon. In fact any delicate, light flower is suitable.

Louis XVI

Balance, simplicity, and pastel tones: this is the style of Louis XVI. And here it is illustrated in an arrangement of garden flowers mixed with wild flowers, and the outline is unbroken. This arrangement needs to be put into the right surroundings. The refined and delicate interiors of the period suit it best. Here it becomes a feature of the general décor.

Container
A Louis XVI chiselled silver urn

Composition

Agapanthas	Larkspur
Blue thistles	Polygonum
White cosmea	Garden roses
Delphiniums	Hollyhocks
Gailliards	Salvia pratensis
White lavatera	Annual scabious
Lupins	Caucasian scabious
Pinks	Orangy-pink zinnias

Method
Place a piece of wire netting or a flower holder in the vase. Put one hollyhock upright in the centre, having removed the lower leaves from the stalk. This is the 'spinal column' of the arrangement.

Begin with the tallest flowers: agapanthas, delphiniums, larkspur, zinnias, then add the medium sized and small flowers grouped at the foot in the centre. Fill up the empty spaces with the remainder of the flowers scattering them throughout. The colours should be dispersed to give a soft and gentle effect. To soften the outline a few flowers should be pulled forward on the rim.

In this arrangement the flowers do not spring from a focal point as in the previous examples. They are set straight in the vase in an upright line.

Variants
The proportions may be modified according to position: if it is placed in the centre of a mantlepiece or, on a console table, it will be broader, but if there are to be two vases framing a central ornament, they will be narrower.

Directoire, Empire

The pyramid shape of this arrangement expresses the rigid style of the Empire period although some freedom in the composition seems to anticipate romanticism. The colours blend with the vase. The flowers have an old world charm. Peonies, roses, lilies and lilac are reminiscent of Redouté, flower painter and teacher of the Empress Josephine at Malmaison.

Container
Etruscan style metal vase painted brown with relief gilding

Composition

Korean chrysanthemums	Forget-me-not
Freesias	Peonies
Narcissi	Prunus
Lilac	Double stocks
Lilies	Ranunculus
Magnolia	Moss roses

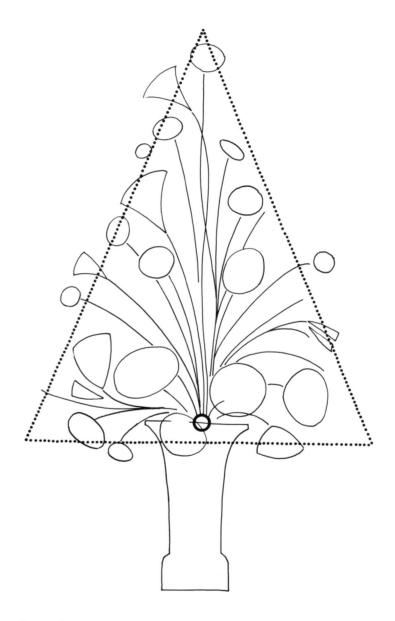

Method
The flower holder should be a lump of Oasis moss rising well above the rim of the vase. It is held in position with netting which is covered with natural moss. This makes it easier to keep the tall flowers steady. First arrange the light and tall flowers: Chrysanthemums, prunus, with a lily and a small rose at the top.

The heavy flowers: peonies, lilies and blown roses are placed close together at the rim.

Finish the arrangement with medium flowers, still keeping the pyramid shape. Fill in the spaces with lilac, and freesias. Arrange some small flowers jutting out over the rim.

Remarks
There are no leaves in this arrangement; all the stems should be stripped at the beginning.

Romantic

This is a mixed arrangement and seems to be without a plan, with garden and wild flowers jumbled haphazardly into the vase. It is a free composition not following basic lines.

To make it successful it needs a profusion of garden flowers, as many varieties as possible. Outdoor flowers like these are abundant during the month of May.

Container
Classical glass goblet with a short stem

Composition

Aquilegia	Forget-me-nots
Hemlock	Narcissi
Wistaria	Apple blossom
Grasses	White roses
Spanish iris	Pyrethrum
Yellow lilies	Tulips
Snapdragons	Viburnum lantana

Method
No flower holders are needed as the arrangement does not follow a plan.

Start by putting a handful of mixed flowers upright in the vase; add the tallest flowers at either side, perhaps a tulip and a white rose. Trail a branch of lilac or apple blossom over the edge of the vase.

A yellow lily and two iris crown the summit of this Spring magic.

Remarks
This type of arrangement is suitable for all kinds of period or modern interiors.

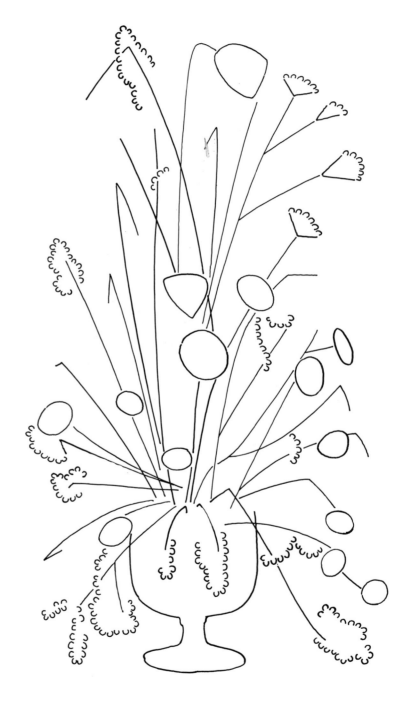

Variation on the theme of the rose

Here is an original way to use full-blown roses, when the petals fall at the slightest touch. It is easy to make but needs a great deal of patience.

Choose a newly opened rose, and strip the petals of a dozen full-blown roses of the same kind into a basket.

Take some very fine wire. Select some fresh and flawless petals of the same size and put them in pairs. Strengthen the tips with a narrow strip of foliage cut from a rose leaf. Stick the wire into the petals and foliage (twist it to hold them) leaving a long end.

Begin by setting a row of petals round the whole rose, winding each wire round the stem and continue increasing the rows of petals; the rows are set lower and lower to attain a rounded effect.

Finish with a row of green leaves, mounted as before on the wire, to form a lacy green collar.

Remarks
Despite its appearance this rose may be kept for several days if carefully wrapped up in slightly damp newspaper every evening.

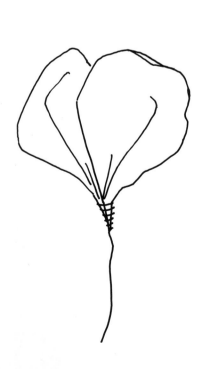

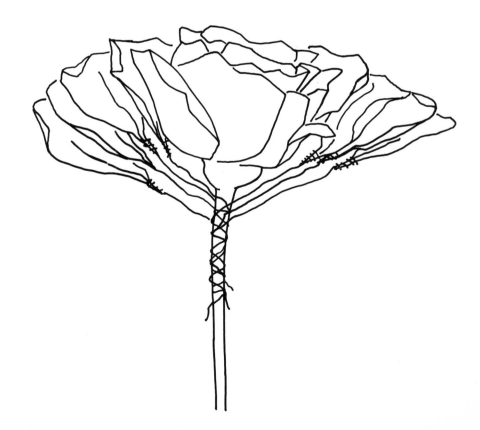

Art nouveau

Scent, fluid lines, gentle arabesques, shaded violet, mauve and white tones evoke the old fashioned elegance of the Belle Epoque. The casually arranged flowers reflect the Japanese influence prevalent in art of the time.

Container
Glass vase with an iris design of the period 1900

Composition
Iris (1)
Wistaria (2)
Lilac (3)
Viburnum carlesii (4)

Method
Choose two branches of lilac of unequal lengths; the tallest should measure one and a half times the height of the vase.
   Cut off the ends crosswise. Cut off any side branches from the main stem leaving only the small leaves. The long branch is placed in centre of the vase, the other slanting to the right with the end of the stalk leaning against the wall of the vase.

   Select one or two branches of wistaria trimming them if need be with the secateurs. The charm of this arrangement is its feeling of movement, which must be carefully preserved.
   Arrange the irises to the right filling up the spaces between the branches. Near the bottom put a slanting branch of viburnum.

Remarks
The flower stalks should not touch the bottom of the vase. Wedged in the neck of the vase, the iris stems can be slanted and so form an integral part of the whole.

Variants
Replace the wistaria with laburnum, the purple with very pale blue iris, the viburnum with honeysuckle. Mixing the perfumes gives an added subtlety to the arrangement.

The Spanish style

Helianthus, a native of Peru, was imported into Europe in the 17th century. There are several varieties popularly known as sunflowers. These brilliant flowers make decorative arrangements, well suited to country styles of Spain or Louis XIII. This design looks best against a plain background – a natural stone wall or dark woodwork.

Container
Copper Louis XIII style pedestal goblet

Composition
Seven sunflowers of different sizes
Yellow coreopsis
Orange-red zinnias

Method
Put the wire netting into the vase and arrange the sunflowers so that they stand well out. This arrangement is looked at from the front and so all the heads must face forward.

Just below the central flower leave a space; this is filled by the leaves of the flower. This lightens the composition. Two heads slanting over the rim of the vase make a splash of colour counterbalanced on the right by a tuft of light coreopsis. Add two orange-coloured zinnias. This vivid note will break up the monochrome effect without destroying the unity of the whole.

Remarks
Leave the leaves on the central stem; the rest are stripped off with the exception of one near the flower.

Variants
Any large flowers, such as dahlias or chrysanthemums, may be used in the same way.

The English style

Sometimes a single flower can inspire a composition. Mrs. Sheila Macqueen, English expert in floral decoration, has chosen for this arrangement arctotis grandis, a large daisy-like star of pure white with a hint of mauve in the centre. The rest of the material, all gathered in the same garden, enhances the delicate beauty of this flower. Delicate touches of pink (magenta rose, hybrid pinks), of yellow (pansy, tobacco-flower), of violet and mauve (clematis, funkia), of grey-green (cineraria maritima), produce a soft and shimmering groundwork.

All harsh outlines and too vivid colours have been omitted on purpose. This arrangement suits the restrained elegance of the Regency period.

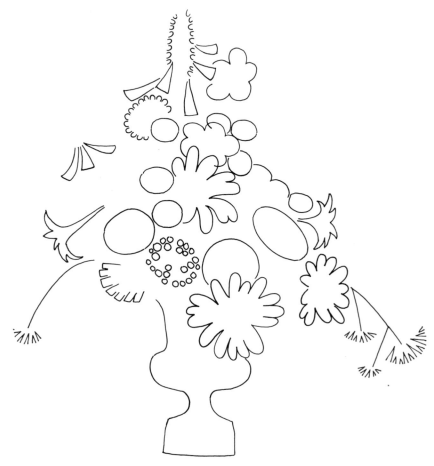

Container
Urn in biscuit porcelain, decorated in relief with gadroons and a garland

Composition

Arctotis grandis	Pansies
Anaphalis margaritacea	Magenta rose
Cineraria maritima	Santolina
Clematis	Sedum spurium coccineum
Funkia	Tobacco-flower
Poppy head	Iberis (candytuft)
Hybrid pinks	

Method
Put a flower holder or a piece of wire netting in the vase. The flowers 'with faces' – arctotis, pinks, pansies, tobacco-flower, and the round ones – rose, anaphalis, candytuft – are grouped in a dense mass. The centre of the composition is an arctotis while two more are prominently placed lower down. A sprig of cineraria maritima, the only foliage to appear in this arrangement, is placed to the left. More delicate flowers, such as funkia or clematis, form the outline of the pyramid shape of the arrangement. Two long stalked sedums fall in a symmetrical line to the base, while an open clematis curves to show its face.

Remarks
Although this arrangement has been carefully composed, with a subtle choice of flowers and colour harmony, it gives a very natural effect.

Decoration on a pedestal

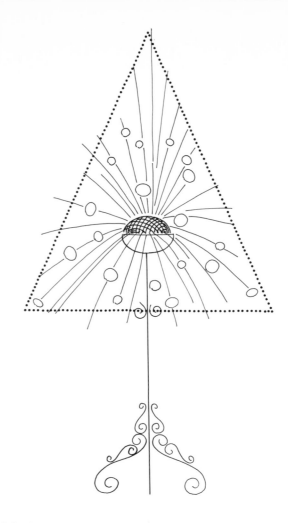

This traditional English arrangement may be used to decorate a church or a reception. It is essentially a show piece, and is usually placed at the end of a room, or in a corner, where it can be seen and admired by visitors. Both flowers and stand harmonize with the style of the furniture and the colouring of the surroundings. A pedestal of wrought iron for instance, would suit a modern interior. For a period room, polished, painted, or gilded wood is preferable. But the essential requirement, whatever the form and material, is absolute stability.

This arrangement, in pastel shades was photographed in the Chapel of the Innocents in Westminster Abbey.

Composition

Astilbe	Stocks
Colvilis	Tagetes
White iris	Tea rose
Genistal (broom)	Solomon's Seal
Wallflower	Spirea
Antirrhinum	

The wrought iron support is surmounted by a terra-cotta bowl fixed firmly at the top. Line the bowl with a piece of Oasis coming well above the top, and cover with a large meshed netting (some of the flowers have big stalks). If necessary, make several holes in the moss with a stick. Outline the structure of the arrangement as to height and width. The tall line is determined by the upright flowers (astilbe, antirrhinum); the low line by the branches of broom falling gracefully downwards. The *focal point,* where the stalks meet, is about a third of the total height.

Finish the arrangement using the remaining flowers. These should radiate outwards from the centre. Those in the front are put in last as they then fit into the moss more easily.

Remarks

The composition is heavy in the centre, and grows lighter towards the edges making the outline soft.

Variants

Experiments in colour can be made with other flowers: blue or white, red or pink, depending on the stand and the setting.

The shape can also be changed. The long and sinuous Hogarth line, the asymmetric, and the triangle are all suitable for this arrangement.

MODERN ARRANGEMENTS

Spring

Iris Susiana, native of Asia, has a lovely dark flower striped with mauve and grey. Jacques Bédat contrasts these handsome flowers with the silver of pussy-willow.

Pebbles continue the grey harmony to the bottom of the glass vase. Three red amaryllis strike a brilliant, heraldic note to celebrate the return of spring.

Container
Cylindrical dish of plain glass

Composition
Amaryllis
Yellow willow catkins (male) and grey (female)
Iris Susiana

Method
Fill the dish with pebbles of varying sizes; they are used as a flower holder. Start with the catkins to define the outline of the arrangement. Put the tallest flowers in the middle, but towards the back, and the others diminishing in length at each side. It is essential that the outline remains light, as if drawn with a very fine brush.

Cut the iris stems to different lengths. Put them in one behind the other in the centre. One flower on the left is almost horizontal, and this breaks up the rather rigid and symmetric effect.

Insert the amaryllis near the rim of the vase; the block of red flowers strikes a vibrant note.

Variants
The effect will be modified by replacing the amaryllis with daffodils. In that case use fewer iris to lighten the composition.

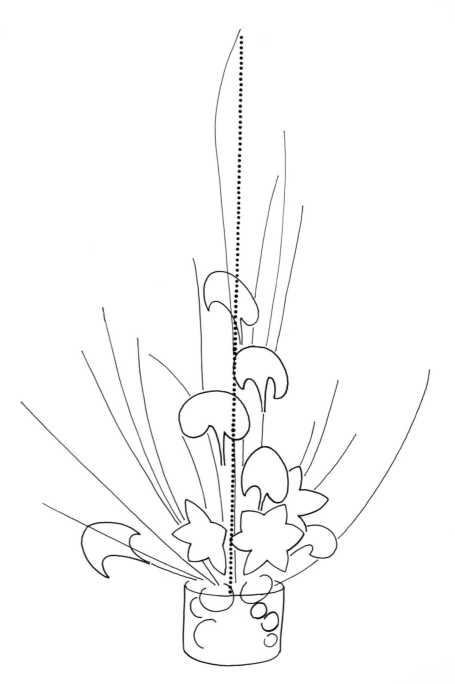

86

Japanese inspiration: spring arrangement

Simplicity, asymmetry and line: these three things are present in most compositions inspired by *Ikebana* (the art of flower decoration in Japan). Western interpretation however is very free, and not subject to the metaphysical ideas of the Orient. This type of arrangement is designed for a modern room decorated with the same restrained simplicity and refinement. The effect would be spoiled by the addition of bright colours.

Container
Wide sandstone vase with a narrow neck. Japanese 16th-century

Composition
Eremurus (1)
Two branches of elm (2)
Philadelphus (3)

Method
The narrow neck of the vase makes a flower holder unnecessary. Put in the eremurus in an upright position, the long stalks curving inwards so that the tips meet. Cut the stems different lengths, and strip them at the bottom.
    Arrange the elm branches round the eremurus, the tallest on the left, the shortest on the right. The latter forms a wider angle with the eremurus than the former. Fill the centre of the arrangement with philadelphus to hide the junction of stems and elm branches.

Remarks
The success of this arrangement depends on its proportions. The slightest alteration disturbs the balance.

Variants
Large foxgloves – branches of sumac – delphiniums – tamarisk.

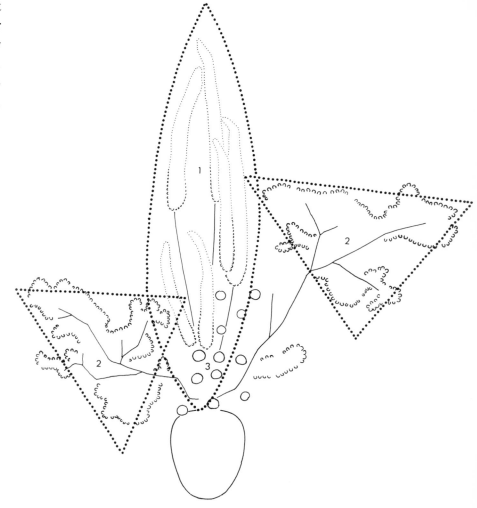

Japanese inspiration: winter

Here again the same principles as have been observed as in the preceding plate: linear movement and restrained colours. Only the idea is different, for it is a winter bouquet, symbolizing the sleep of nature.

The arrangement should be set against a light coloured background. There should be nothing nearby to interrupt the soaring branches. Here it is placed on the ground in front of a bare wall, but it could stand on a long, low sideboard. Turn the vase slightly to the left so that the curve of the principal branch comes forward giving a harmonious line to the whole.

Container
Culos pottery bottle, reminiscent of a Japanese *sake* bottle

Composition
Black thorn covered in grey lichen (1)
Yarrow (2)

Method
The design is determined by the natural form of the branches. If necessary, remove some branches to accentuate the clear outline. Strip the bottom of the stem as the neck of the bottle is narrow.

Insert the first branch leaning towards the right. Place the smaller branches round it and angle them to the left; two curve outwards to the right near the bottom, and the final one is angled sharply downwards.

Arrange the yarrow in the space between the branches; the shortest ones close to the rim of the vase.

Remarks
The whole arrangement leans to the right in a balanced, asymmetric movement.

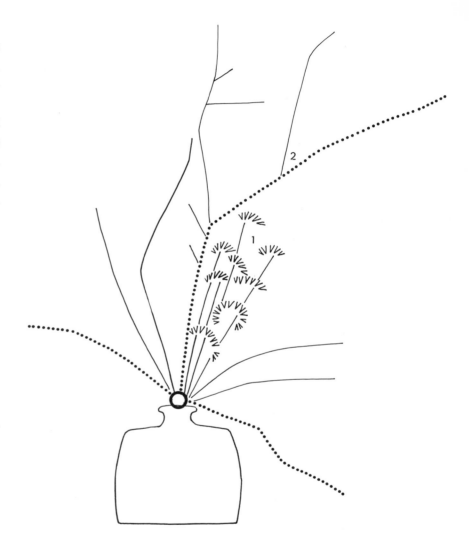

Variants
The choice of material depends on the seasons:
Spring: apple blossom with three peonies at the base
Summer: tamarisk and hydrangeas in pink tones
Autumn: cotoneaster with three chrysanthemums
Winter: larch with three Christmas roses

Japanese inspiration: flowers and driftwood

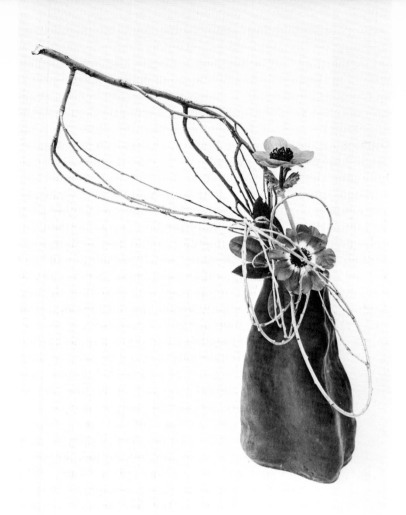

These twisting tree stumps, polished smooth by the water, are sometimes found by the sea shore or on river banks. They look like strange, bold, rhythmical carvings. The Japanese combine them with flowers and foliage in symbolic compositions widely imitated in the West today. This very free interpretation, however, has no symbolism.

Composition
Madonna lilies
Funkia and saxifrage leaves
A gnarled driftwood

Method
Put the trunk on a flat piece of bark, and if necessary fix it with a nail or plasticine. At its foot stand a small, low bowl fitted with a pinholder. Arrange the funkia and saxifrage leaves round the rim, and put in two lilies, one taller than the other, in the centre.

Put a glass tube into the hollow part of the trunk. Fill it with water, and put in two more lilies to make the top of the arrangement.

Remarks
The lilies follow the line of the trunk.

The nage-ire style

The interest of this decoration lies in the spatial movement and line. Its extreme simplicity is typical of the *nage-ire* style.

Container
Stoneware vase in the shape of a rock

Composition
Anemones   Camelia leaves   Willow

Method
Arrange the willow branch in the curves required and insert it quickly into the vase. Put one anemone and three camelia leaves close to the rim of the vase and another anemone a little higher.

Variants
The willow can be replaced by any kind of pliant branches such as vines, stauntonia, clematis, ivy; the anemones can be interchanged with chrysanthemums, roses, camelias, cymbidiums or carnations.

92

Scandinavian taste: the vase an integral part of the composition

This poetic arrangement echoes the awakening of Spring after the long, northern winter; it is like the grey reflections of the sky in a rippling little lake. Once again Japanese influence can be seen in the line of this arrangement.

Container
Lobed glass bowl, designed by the Finnish architect, Alvar Aalto

Composition
A large branch of black-thorn
White narcissi
Grey pebbles

Method
Fill the bowl to a quarter of its height as bulbous flowers, narcissi, tulips like only a little water.

Put the branch of black-thorn to the right, and fix it in one of the lobes to keep it steady.

Put in the pebbles to hold the flowers. Cut the stems of the narcissi in diminishing lengths so that they form a continuous line right down to the level of the water.

Remarks
The black-thorn curves to the left in a continuous, graceful line.

Variants
Instead of the narcissi use flag iris and replace the black-thorn with a flowering branch, such as apple blossom or forsythia.

Designed by first-rate artists, many modern vases are beautiful in their own right. The material and shape dictate to some extent the choice of flowers and the style of the arrangement. The vase is now not only useful but an integral part of the whole design. Here are two arrangements designed for very different vases.

Containers
A trilobial cylinder in polished matt steel
At the side an identical but shallower container

Composition
Amaryllis
Two branches of cherry blossom, one very long and one short
Two small branches of prunus

Method
Insert the long cherry blossom branch in one of the lobes, and the amaryllis in another. The two amaryllis create a solid mass to balance the stark effect of the cherry blossom. Two small prunus branches, with a strong curving line, break the contour and soften the vertical, slightly stiff line of the arrangement.

The small vase is a miniature repetition of the larger arrangement. The two together make a harmonious composition.

Remarks
Perceptive distribution of line, volume and space has created this beautiful composition.

Scandinavian taste: spring flowers

Here is simplicity in a spring composition, and it is easy to make. It is a design of contrasts, light and shade, like the spring after a hard winter. The arrangement follows a slightly asymmetrical line.

Container
A quadrangular Finnish bowl of thick glass

Composition
White narcissi
Euphorbia

Method
No flower holder is needed. The narcissi, of different lengths, are arranged on the left of the bowl with the shorter ones leaning over the edge. On the right the bunch of euphorbia counterbalances the narcissi. One branch juts out horizontally.

Remarks
The centres of the narcissi pick up the orange of the euphorbia flowers, subtly enhancing the effect of the whole.

Variants
White iris – Black tulips
Blue hyacinths – White lilac
White marguerites – Buddleia

Scandinavian taste: simplicity and line

This arrangement is a study of the graphic outline of the strelitzia. The flowers look like strange birds with slender wings.
The two branches of euphorbia at the base are the counter-
point of the colour harmony – green and vermilion red.

Container
Finnish vase in the shape of a candlestick. Various shapes of Scandinavian vases can be used for this kind of arrangement

Composition
Three strelitzias
Two branches of euphorbia

Method
Choose the longest stem of strelitzia, it should be about three
times the height of the vase. Place it so that the stalk touches
the bottom so forming a straight unbroken line. Insert the
second stem in front of the first, turning the flower to the left.
It should come about half way up in the arrangement.

  Put in the branches of euphorbia on either side; the one on
the right obliquely, the other slightly curved. This asymmetric line is necessary to achieve a proper balance.

  This arrangement looks more effective against a pale background.

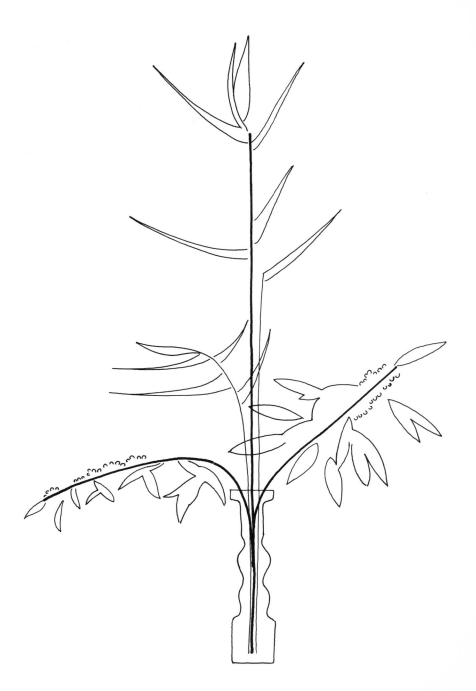

Scandinavian taste: Japanese influence

The careful choice of the materials, and the twisting shape of the branches make this a very attractive arrangement. The experienced eye will see the subtle contrast between heavier and lighter shapes. This restrained style, full of nuances, is the basis of Japanese floral art.

Container
Handmade unglazed jar

Composition
A dead branch or some driftwood
A branch of aubergine
A tuft of sedum
A rosette of crassula

Method
Set the branch and the aubergines in an upright position, adjusting them so that their curves form an attractive pattern. Remove leaves if necessary as the balance of the arrangement depends on a light, elegant line.

Put in a tuft of sedum and then the rosette of crassula. The purplish glint of the leaves picks up the colour of the aubergines, while the grey stump suits the texture of the stoneware vase.

Remarks
This arrangement would be suitable for a kitchen decoration but it would not be out of place in a modern living room with simple furniture and plain walls.

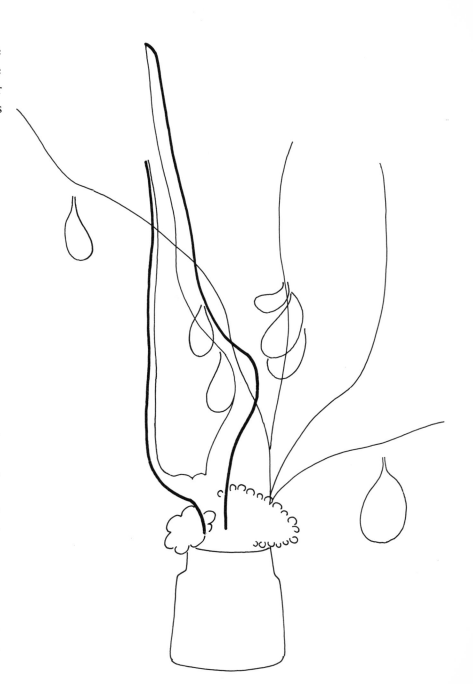

ARRANGEMENTS IN THEIR SETTINGS

Contrast

Giant flowers in front of an arabesque background. This traditional French arrangement is made to reflect nature; large trees reach towards the sky in contrast to the tiny flowers growing in the shade of the undergrowth. Between these two extremes the flowers are arranged in order of size and height. This is shown here in a period arrangement created for rich 18th-century setting. The very tall flowers enhance the decorative elegance of a Louis XV screen.

Container
Silver-gilt wine cooler, early 18th century

Composition
Delphiniums
Eremurus
Auratum lilies
Pansies

Method
Fit into the vase a large piece of synthetic moss; it should be higher than the rim. Cover it with wire netting to hold it firmly.

Put in the centre, but towards the back, the tallest stem of eremurus, placing it slightly to the right. Arrange the other flowers in diminishing order of height allowing the stems to cross in the centre of the arrangement. The composition is slightly asymmetrical; working alternately from left to right will help to maintain this shape.

Four auratum lilies are grouped low down near the rim: the fifth is placed a little higher on the left.

The small pansies are put into the neck of the vase and allowed to be bend naturally over the rim. This homely touch relieves the solemnity of the composition.

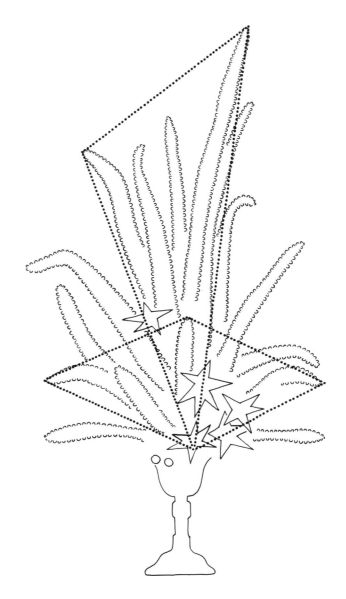

Remarks
This majestic arrangement is only suitable for a tall, spacious reception room. Its decorative and powerful lines would suit the corner of a salon.

The flowers repeat the dominant colours of the décor

A Louis XV tapestry, with warm but subdued colours is the principal feature of the room. The arrangement picks up the shades of the tapestry but in brighter colours. Its purpose is not to intrude, but to enliven the traditional and rather restrained surroundings. Apart from the two amaryllis, the arrangement contains only garden flowers; it is a splendid arrangement in the 18th-century manner.

Container
A gold ewer of the 17th century

Composition

Amaryllis	Auratum lily
Alstromeria	Tiger lily
Campanula Carpathica	Larkspur
Campanula Pyramidale	Red and pink peonies
Gerberas	Caladium leaves

Method
Put a spiked flower holder in the bottom of the vase and make a wire netting mould to fit it.

The tallest flowers – the orange tiger lilies, and the alstromeria – are set upright in the vase to form the body of the arrangement. Near them, but on a lower level angle a stem of two auratum lilies.

Fill out the base with the larger flowers – peonies and amaryllis. Put in several gerberas and a tiger lily, blending the colours. Below the amaryllis a leaf of caladium curves downwards gracefully and a few small flowers bend over the edge of the vase.

Remarks
The colours are the feature of this arrangement: its success depends on harmonizing them well. Step back from time to time as you make this arrangement, and judge the effect from a distance.

Working on the same principle, i.e., a massed effect, the alternate use of heavy and slender flowers will make it possible to vary the colour scheme to suit a different setting.

Two arrangements for a man of taste

A sense of elegance implies a sense of harmony. Harmony of shapes, colours, and materials. This gift is inherent in a great *couturier*, and it is not only confined to his profession. Pierre Balmain uses his taste and talents just as happily in other fields. The two flower arrangements shown here were done by him in his apartment. The simple flowers are arranged without affectation, but with characteristic skill. They add the warm poetic note which animates a room.

Harmony en camaïeu

Composition
Three tiger lilies in a spherical glass vase
Orange-coloured lilies combine with natural oak panelling and the collection of antique terra-cotta arranged in a niche, against a background of blue grey velvet.

Red harmony

This is a very classic fan-shaped arrangement placed under a charming 18th-century painting. Round flowers are grouped together in the middle while the long, slender ones form the outline. The various tones blend with the colours in the painting and the crimson damask hangings.

Composition	
Garlic flowers	White lilies
Ears of wheat	White marguerites
Coreopsis	Garden tea roses
Pink and red gladioli	Polyanthus roses 'Alain'
	Bull rushes

Remarks

This arrangement is predominantly red. To attain this effect the chosen colour must be put in the centre of the composition – in this case the red polyanthus roses – it then becomes the focal point.

Flowers and a fireplace

A large arrangement like this is very suitable to hide an empty grate in the summer. Spread out like a fan in front of a tiled fireplace it also hides a rather ugly fire screen. Mrs. Julia Clements has chosen garden flowers to match the *Delft* blue and white tiles. On a hot summer's day the decoration has a cool effect which enhances the charm of the composition.

Container
A wide-mouthed ceramic vase

Composition
Campanula
Delphiniums
Ferns
Pyrethrum

Method
For arrangements that are worked from the centre it is always best to use synthetic moss. Mould it up to the top of the vase, and cover it with netting, it makes it easier to arrange the flowers quickly and firmly. To put in the larger stalks more easily, pierce holes in the moss with a wooden stick of a size smaller than the stems.

As it is to be placed at ground level the arrangement will nearly always be viewed from above and may appear squat. To obviate this, it is essential that the principal flower should be much taller than in other arrangements. Here a tall delphinium stands well above the mass of flowers.

The falling line at the base is formed by two symmetrical, slanting delphiniums. Fill in the arrangement with flowers of different lengths. Always begin from the centre and work outwards in a fan shape. (See sketch.)

Group the pyrethrums and some campanulas in the centre of the composition. Allow some space for the white campanulas to show up among the delphiniums. The ferns add a touch of green.

Remarks
Some of the flowers project in the front and give a depth to the whole. The back, which is not seen, is flat.

Variants
Replace the delphiniums by hollyhocks, gladioli or fox gloves; the pyrethrums with round flowers such as peonies, roses, dahlias, chrysanthemums or hydrangeas.

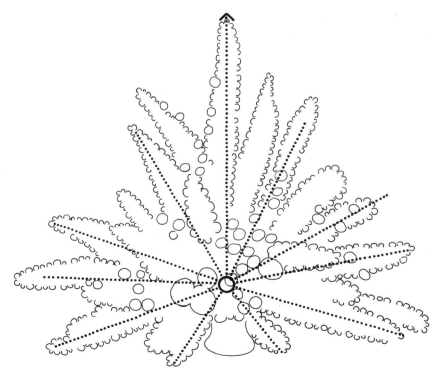

Architectural arrangement

The line is slender, asymmetrical, with rhythmic use of bright, contrasting colours. The flowers are grouped together, or spaced singly above and below the rim of a cylindrical vase. This arrangement stands out well in a modern setting in neutral colours. Make sure that ornaments of equal size are moved away as they destroy the effect.

Container
Cylindrical vase in a neutral colour

Composition
Purple Berberis Thunbergii	Antirrhinums
Gerberas	Blue pansies
Auratum lily	Viburnum
Orange lily	

Method
Begin with the main line of the arrangement; put in the tallest flowers (antirrhinums, lilium auratum) so that they are well spread out.

Put the blue pansies and the orange lilies near the rim to form the compact brilliant mass which is the heart of the arrangement.

Finish by filling with branches of viburnum, berberis and some antirrhinums, retaining the shape of the arrangement. A long low branch placed on the right prolongs the subtle, asymmetric line of the design.

Remarks
This kind of arrangement should not be placed against a wall, it needs plenty of space round it. It is made to be seen from all sides.

Variants
This type of cylindrical vase is suitable for any slender compositions of tall flowers such as delphiniums, gladioli, or lupins.

Flowers and books

A space between shelves is possibly the excuse to design a small still life to break the monotony of the straight line. This brilliant arrangement of Spring flowers makes a contrast to the dark background of the bookshelves. Books and decorative objects complement this young, up-to-date decoration.

Container
White ceramic bowl, very modern in shape

Composition
Box
Dyed broom
Gerbera
Daffodils
White and yellow narcissi

Method

First make the rounded outline with branches of box and broom. Then put in the daffodils cutting them progressively shorter. The centre is formed by a cross of white narcissus; they give a light appearance at the focal point.

The gerberas, on the other hand, come well forward. Singling them out in this way gives more impact to the shape of the flowers and enlivens the arrangement.

Remarks

The back of the bouquet is flat, so that the vase fits into the shelves.

Variants

This still life can be repeated easily, depending on inspiration and the flowers available. Try to create a contrast between the flowers, the vase and the background: green background, orange marigolds, black vase; pale blue background, red roses, siver goblet; bright blue background, white flowers, transparent glass vase.

Bishopthorpe Palace

For seven hundred years Archbishops of York have lived at Bishopthorpe Palace. The austere building lacks neither comfort nor amenities. Flowered chintz curtains frame the gothic windows overlooking the romantic English countryside. A perfect picture of the traditional English way of life.

The large arrangement on a stand is particularly suitable for this fine room. The lines of this majestic arrangement flow without constraint. George Smith has created a vibrant composition which enlivens the subdued tones of the room.

The pedestal, a *torchère* of carved dark wood, is a good contrast to the brilliant flowers.

Composition

Buddleia Davidii magnifica	Hydrangeas
Dahlias	Liatris
Gladioli	Carnations
Copper beech	Roses

Method

On the top of the stand there is a deep metal bowl, filled with synthetic moss strengthened with wire netting.

The gladioli in the centre form the axis. The longest is twice the height of the stand. The longest stems are in bud; open flowers would probably bend under their own weight.

The falling line below is formed by two branches of copper beech, one slightly longer than the other.

The central part of the arrangement, radiating from the focal point consists of: red roses, dahlias, hydrangeas and carnations grouped in a solid mass. From the centre outwards the flowers become increasingly widespread. The tall slender flowers – buddleia and gladioli – define the outline, and they all converge to the same point.

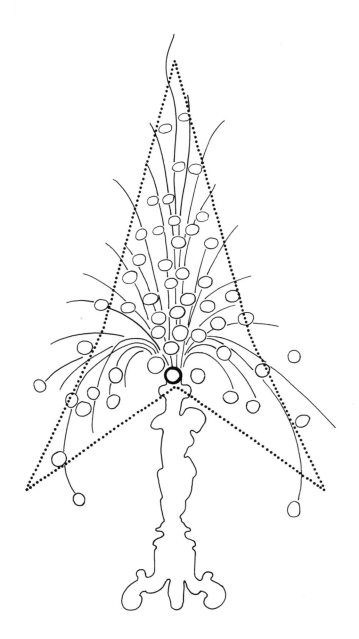

Harmony en camaïeu, warm tones

An arrangement of variegated colours does not necessarily give the impression or the feeling of warmth which is generally associated with vivid colours. Flowers of various tones make for a more subtle and original composition. In this case the effect is created in a palette which ranges from bright yellow to dark violet with a dominant orange binding it into a vibrant whole.

Container
Rough stoneware pot

Composition
Yellow, orange and purple chrysanthemums
Red roses
Pyracantha, leaves and berries

Method
The arrangement should be constructed like a cube, to be seen from all sides, and the flowers are placed naturally so as to form blocks of vivid colour in a luminous whole. The rich colours should be grouped in the centre; red roses, purple chrysanthemums on a background of dark leaves. The other flowers radiate round, whilst a bunch of pyracantha berries hangs over the edge of the pot and another branch mingles with the orange chrysanthemums at the top. Yellow chrysanthemums form blocks of colour here and there. A larger one stands free, above the arrangement. Now add a few branches of pyracantha, their delicate leaves and the pliant line of the stems will avoid a rigid effect.

Remarks
The dark foliage is an indispensable factor for success, forming a contrast which throws the flower colours into relief.

Variants
Garden tea-roses, tiger lilies, copper beech

Harmony en camaïeu, cool tones

Sometimes the vase is as much a part of the composition as the flowers. The two parts unite to form a single whole. This rule only applies to vases of distinction which are also used as ornaments: a Chinese Sung vase, opaline glass, or a piece of fine quality modern glass, for instance.

Container
Cylindrical vase of ground glass in shaded tones of blue and violet

Composition
White anemones with violet centres
White and mauve iris
Two decorative leaves of curly Kale

Method
The anemones and iris are paler than the shadowy tones of the vase. To make the blue, the deep violet and the delicate white stand out, a strong colour is needed; in this case the purple anemone in the centre.

The anemones are grouped irregularly in the centre, the more open ones being an inch or two higher, then come the iris, their elegant heads soaring above.

The two symmetrical 'ears' jutting from the edge are striped green and pink cabbage leaves.

Remarks
This type of arrangement goes well in a modern setting against a light, neutral background. Strong colours would kill its soft shaded tones.

TABLES, FESTIVALS AND RECEPTIONS

To invite a friend is to be responsible for his happiness during the whole time he spends under your roof.

Brillat-Savarin, *The Physiology of Taste*

Brillat-Savarin was as good a psychologist as he was an epicure: for a gourmet good food is not enough. The whole setting must also be warm and receptive with a well-dressed table. Nothing is more boring than the 'perfect dinner' served on a classic table, or the rich conventional buffet of the caterer. The hostess must have imagination, and the decoration of the dinner table, like a room, must reflect not only a personality but a state of mind.

Whether it is a formal dinner or a buffet party, the type of reception is determined by the style of living and the character of the room. A gentleman farmer in the Highlands entertains in a very different manner from an artist in an attic in Montparnasse. The essential thing is to be oneself, and to offer simply what one has.

A pot-au-feu served in an earthenware soup tureen is just as good as a lobster served on Sèvres porcelain.

The principal object is harmony:

Check tablecloths or modern pottery are unsuitable in an 18th-century setting. On the other hand, fine silver and china on a lace tablecloth are out of place in a country cottage.

Paradoxically the fine things of the past are admissible in the best modern settings, but the contrast fails if the materials are second rate.

It is said that flowers are the smile of a well-set table. But the smile must be natural, without effort. The first rule is that the flowers must fit with the setting; the table linen, plates, cutlery and décor of the dining room.

Avoid:

Too many flowers. A table is not a garden.

Too heavily scented flowers. Guests cannot enjoy the smell of game and hyacinths at the same time.

Flowers which fade quickly, especially when they are arranged on the cloth. Nothing is more depressing than fading flowers with the dessert.

Exotic flowers of unusual shape (strelitzias, anthuriums) with simple pottery and ordinary glasses.

Country flowers in a rich setting although certain kinds of wild plants, flowers, herbs and branches will fit well in some rich settings.

Tall and bushy arrangements irritating for guests sitting opposite each other. As a rule, the decoration should not be more than twelve inches tall.

Remember that a table decoration has to be seen from all sides.

Flowers and objets d'art: Bright-coloured anemones in a metal vase surround a silver duck (East India Company, 18th century). This very pretty table decoration does not interfere with guests seated opposite

Experiment with colours:

Contrasts make a table look gay; softness and subtlety are achieved with tones of the same colour.

Avoid mixed flowers on an embroidered cloth. Choose the dominant colour for a monochrome arrangement. It will stand out to greater effect. A plain cloth allows infinite choice. Look for affinities or contrasts in colour with the principle elements of the setting: cloth, napkins, china and flowers. Here are some suggestions:

White cloth, white and gold plates . . . . Red flowers; amaryllis, carnations, peonies, or roses

White cloth, turquoise plates . . . . Yellow flowers; iris, daffodils, tulips

Bright blue cloth, white plates . . . . White flowers; marguerites, peonies, roses, or white and blue flowers mixed, marguerites and corn-flowers

Pastel blue cloth, white plates . . . . Orange flowers; tiger lilies, marigolds, dahlias

Red cloth, white napkins . . . . White flowers, green plants (ivy, grasses, foliage) Fruit and vegetables

Pale pink cloth, blue and white plates . . . . Blue forget-me-nots, or mixed anemones
of Chinese porcelain or *Delft*

Yellow cloth, blue plates . . . . Blue and yellow iris

Dark green cloth, white plates . . . . Orange marigolds, or russet leaves, chrysanthemums or fruit

Each place can be an arrangement in itself if one uses modern place settings. Use a small cloth with contrasting napkins, and stress the colour contrast between plates or glasses. If each place is to have an individual arrangement, pick up one or two of the colours in the flowers.

Toast coloured linen mats, orange . . . . Marigolds (or gerberas)
napkins, white plates

Red mats, blue napkins, white plates . . . . Cornflowers, or marguerites mixed with cornflowers

Bright blue mats and napkins, yellow . . . . Primroses, daffodils,
plates pansies

Central motif: pompom dahlias, six candles

Detail of a banquet. Every place setting has a pink and green candle stuck in a pineapple

One could go on for ever, the possibilities are endless. Some hostesses go still further in their search for harmony. It is said that Mrs. Roosevelt liked to decorate her table with blue delphiniums matching the colour of her eyes! A small posy on the napkin – sometimes just a single flower – is a charming touch greatly appreciated by guests.

Flowers and objects

The classic arrangements of former days, figured baroque and rococo vases overloaded with flowers and fruit, have almost disappeared from the table and been replaced by an objet d'art such as a soup-tureen, remnant of a precious service, which becomes the central ornament. Or it might be a silver duck, an East India Company *terrine,* floating on a sea of anemones; small terra-cotta figures, cupids, or dancers, marble obelisk, or glass columns linked by garlands; a pewter goblet with red roses; or coloured stones mingled with exotic flowers.

One does not always possess a valuable piece. A pretty shell filled with flowers, or an arrangement of shells, flowers and aquatic plants is just as attractive. I have even seen an aquarium with goldfish in it as the centre piece of an imaginative and charming under-water décor of coral, shells and water plants.

Flowers, fruit and vegetables

Any natural products mix well. The history of painting shows many examples, from the ancient Pompeian frescoes to the characters from Arcimboldo. But it is only in the 18th century that still life gained favour among artists of countries such as France, Holland, Spain, Italy. Their handsome creations full of inspiration and an inexhaustible source of ideas.

Choose fruit and vegetables of different shapes and colours for contrast. All art consists of the balance of tonal values. Even an ordinary turnip becomes interesting beside a red pimento, or a tomato. Put a shiny green pepper with a pink velvety peach, a contrast of black grapes with white mushrooms. Strawberry leaves and spirea will help to lighten a too solid mass.

Choose colours in harmony with the decoration of the table and the room. In a period setting – where there is dark woodwork and pewter, use clear colours, green, red, black and white. Yellow and orange tones enliven a neutral background.

These bunches of vegetables fit naturally into the brightness of a modern kitchen, where family meals are served nowadays. Their presence is proof that the simplification of daily life does not mean that all aesthetic pleasures have to be abandoned.

Arrangement of vegetables

The simplest vegetables, carrots, lettuce, turnips, leeks and so on, have a far from negligible decorative effect. Their colours and shapes are varied and lend themselves to country compositions. This one, actually made for a kitchen, would look just as well on a table or sideboard in the country.

Composition

Artichokes	Grean beans
Asparagus	Lettuce
Aubergines	Turnips
Carrots	Onions
White mushrooms	Red and green tomatoes
Lemons	Two branches of ivy

Method

Spread a layer of modelling clay or plasticine on a rectangular wooden base. Put a pinholder in the centre.

Start with the long pieces, asparagus, ivy branches, which will determine the line. Two lettuce heads form the heart of the arrangement. Distribute the other vegetables by alternating volume and colour. If necessary fasten them together with a small pointed piece of wood (sharpened matches for example) as this will help to reinforce the arrangement.

Fill the spaces with small bunches of green beans attached with wire.

Variants

Other vegetables can be chosen: cabbage, cauliflower, cucumber, celery, melons or leeks. Narrow and long shapes should be alternated with round and solid shapes.

Festivals

However far we go back into the past we find flowers linked with every religious and profane rite, every festival and spectacle. The Greeks decorated their houses and temples with garlands of flowers, while every spring the Romans held the *Rosaria* – festival of the roses. The difficulty today is to decide what is fitting for the occasion.

Baptism
Although simple and gay, the table at a christening is formal, with white cloth, fine porcelain and antique silver. Pomposity is however to be avoided. Choose flowers that are pastel coloured: lilies-of-the-valley, hyacinths, white lilies, pink lilies, peonies, roses, delphiniums, marguerites, spring flowers, and garden flowers. Dragées (coloured sugared almonds) arranged on the table or in bowls pick up the tones.

If you prefer fantasy rather than tradition, here is an amusing idea: a large round light green cabbage with the centre removed and filled with flowers such as sweet peas, marguerites, anemones.

Wedding
A sophisticated and luxurious design is suitable. Use an embroidered or lace cloth, fine porcelain and antique silver. Ostentatious display, lacking the restraint of real elegance, should be avoided and also the conventional pure white lilies or gladioli.

Nowadays a few pastel colours are increasingly mixed with the white: pale blue delphiniums, pink odontoglossums, or blue primula. Hot-house flowers (orchids, phalaenopsis or cattleyas) are only suitable for banquets.

Dark and very strong colours such as purple, orange, yellow, dark blue or violet should be avoided.

Golden weddings
Golden weddings are celebrated with the ceremonial due to fifty years of marriage. There should be no sad or melancholy associations. Everything should induce a feeling of warmth and well-being: a cloth embroidered with gold thread, gleaming silver and fine porcelain. Symbolically a gold chain winds like a serpent the length of the table. In the centre a basket overflowing with golden ears of corn and brilliant flowers: gerberas, antirrhinums, Korean chrysanthemums, freesias, lilium auratum, tulips, daffodils, tea roses. It should be as golden as the setting sun.

Place a bunch of violets in a golden bowl – a touch of warmth and affection – in front of the guests of honour.

Easter
The spring festival should be celebrated with seasonal flowers rather than hot-house blooms. A joyous harmony should express the happiness of spring. Use strong touches of colour, bright red gerberas, yellow-gold pansies, to heighten the fresh tints of the spring flowers: forget-me-nots, apple blossom, and daisies. Eggs, symbol of Easter, may be placed among the flowers as here, but they should be dyed to match the flowers.

Christmas
Tradition determines the Christmas decorative theme in most Western countries: pine, holly, garlands, shining gold and silver balls. Christmas is essentially the children's festival and they love these decorations. Not only the table but the whole room can be decorated: with pine on the chimney-piece, mixed garlands of holly, pine and iridescent glass balls hanging festooned on the walls and round the doors and windows.

Single motif: holly, Christmas roses, candle

The table will be gay and sumptuous. There should be a good deal of gold and silver, bright colours and shining reflections. It is a warm welcoming festival. So increase the candles for candlelight is as becoming to people's faces as it is to the other things, especially silver. In a small terra-cotta bowl, place three Christmas roses and a few sprigs of holly, adding a candle in the centre. Place one in front of every guest, alternating white and red or pink and green candles. One can also use a grapefruit, an orange or apple as a candle-holder.

The table centre matches the individual bouquets. Here are some suggestions:

Gold cloth:	Yellow flowers with gilded leaves
	or red flowers with green foliage
Silver cloth:	White flowers with silver foliage
	or orange flowers with green foliage
Red cloth:	Red flowers with green foliage

To escape from tradition, Jacques Bédat suggests an exotic Christmas which has the special character of a grand occasion. Palm leaves, pineapples and hot-house flowers give the festival an Oriental character without destroying its poetic mystery. In the south – Italy, for instance – this mixture is quite usual. Pine and ears of corn mingle with fruit. Apples, oranges, lemons, grapefruit, grapes, pomegranates, provide the motifs for heavy garlands. For might not the shepherds and the Magi have brought these same fruits on that first Christmas night?

Decoration for a table must fit the shape and size of the table

Round or square table: two places

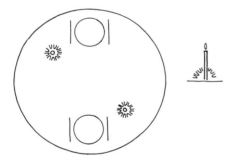

Small arrangement placed at the side

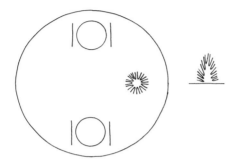

Two motifs, flowers and candle, set at the right of each plate

Small table: four to six places

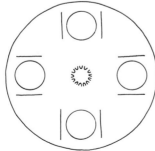

One central bouquet

Large table: four to six places

One central arrangement with garlands between each setting

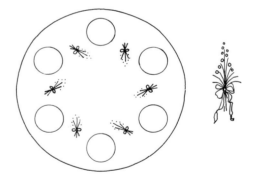

Six small bouquets, one set in front of each guest

One candelabra (or decorative object) surrounded by small bouquets

Long table (oval or rectangular) : eight to twelve places

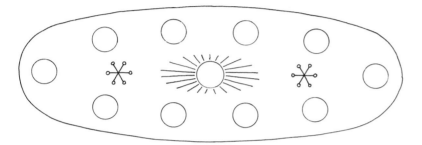

A large tureen in the centre with flowers and two candelabras

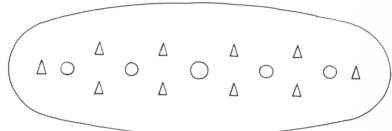

A French style table decorated with alternate pyramids and balls

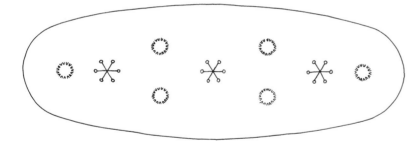

Three candelabras and six small flower motifs

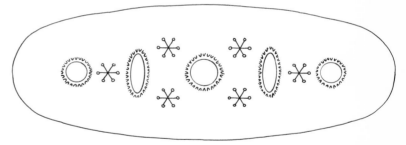

One soup tureen in the centre; two sauce boats decorated with flowers; two trays of fruit at the ends of the table; six candelabras distributed between the motifs

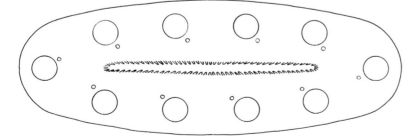

A very long central motif. Flowers and a candle in front of each guest

Fruit, flowers, foliage, vegetables and grasses in a pewter mug call to mind a still life of the 17th century. A tall lily dominates the arrangement. This table decoration fits well in a period setting; on a polished oak table, with pewter goblets and plates, and dark mats.

Composition

Oats and wheat	Wild strawberries in flower
Judas tree	White lily
Artichokes	Lichees
Cherries	White lilac
Green lemons	Cut melon
Cow parsley	Peppers
Cultivated mushrooms	Tomatoes
Courgettes (baby marrow)	Viburnum
Caladium leaves	

Method

Shape the wire netting into a cone over the mug. Its height should equal that of the vase. Cover this with natural moss.

Attach the biggest fruits and vegetables with a small piece of wire fixed to the end of each one: the lemons and several others may simply be pinned on.

Arrange the fruit and vegetables in alternating colours over the whole surface of the cone.

Between each group insert the lighter fruits such as cherry and lichees, and also the flowering branches and grasses. One branch slants to the left and is hung with cherries, a charmingly natural touch.

Put the lily among the grasses at the top. A happy distribution of colour and of shape is essential. Delicate touches of white – lilac, viburnum lantana and flowering strawberries – enliven the arrangement.

Remarks

Instead of a pewter mug, use a piece of early pottery, a soup tureen, a vegetable dish or country bowl. Every kind of fruit and vegetable can be used according to season, climate and imagination. For instance, the courgettes may be exchanged for aubergines; lemons for pomegranates, cherries for gooseberries or a bunch of grapes.

18th century

The table is set in the dining room of M. Pierre Balmain. The room is white with small touches of colour. Blue and white Chinese porcelain fills the corner cabinets, the wall sconces are Louis XVI gilt bronze, while the chairs are covered in brownish red leather.

The dinner table repeats the same subtle harmony: white tablecloth, Chinese *famille rose* plates, cut crystal glasses. The white decoration enhances the elegant décor.

Composition
White marguerites with yellow centres
Gypsophila paniculata
Bullrushes

Method
The daisies form the heart of the composition while the gypsophila surrounds it with a misty cloud. The whole arrangement is delicate and light.

Take two bullrushes, one longer than the other, and put them in the centre.

Remarks
Do not overcrowd the daisies; each head must stand out clearly. They should be arranged at different levels to give a dimensional effect.

Greenery and rock work

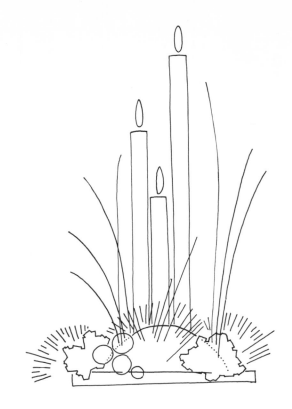

Dinner by candlelight in one of the great salons of Paris. The atmosphere is warm: red napery and crimson damask accented with gold. Each table is decorated with a rococo design in the style of the 18th century. Woodland plants, grasses, wild and garden flowers emerge from stones arranged to look like a rockery. White candles softly light the room. Underneath each decoration is a plain wooden or metal tray.

Composition
Strawberry plants with flowers and fruit (wild strawberries or the variety known as 'Four Seasons')
Grasses, wild flowers, fern
Wild pinks
Sweet Williams
Moss roses
Stones of different shapes and sizes

Method
Stick the stones on the tray with some modelling clay leaving enough space for three to five candles of different heights.

Fill up the spaces between the stones with synthetic moss soaked in water, and cover with flat, natural moss.

Plant the strawberries and their roots in the damp moss.

Here and there add the grasses, ferns, a sweet william, a moss rose, and a bunch of wild pinks... Avoid a formal arrangement it should suggest a wild and poetic garden.

Remarks
Be sparing with heavy flowers, rather increase the wild flowers for a delicate effect.

Variants
Change the composition according to the season or climate:
Spring: Shells, seaweed, water flowers
Summer: Field flowers, raspberries, gooseberries and all the small garden fruits, butterflies
Autumn: Mushrooms, autumn leaves, wild bay leaves

Decoration for a mantelpiece

In the same salon (see preceding page), the fireplace takes up the decorative theme of the tables. Two luxuriant rococo designs at each end of the salon bring life to the noble Louis XVI décor: panelling with classical pilasters, white marble mantlepiece carved with rosette motifs. Plants and flowers, in red and green tones with touches of white, harmonize with the setting. It is a fine example of a creation by Jacques Bédat based on an idea by Jean-François Daigre.

Composition
Rocky stones chosen specially for the decoration
Amaryllis
Strawberry plant (flowers and fruit)
Grasses
Greenhouse plants in pots; flowering cactus, caladium, chlorophytum
White flowered clerodendron, nephrolepis, tri-coloured nidularium

Method
Make two pyramids of stones and leave enough space between for the flower pots.

Insert the stalks of amaryllis into glass tubes filled with water. Put some damp moss around the roots of the strawberry plants: press it down and enclose them in small plastic bags. They will remain fresh for a long time.

A plume of grasses crowns the design on the left. On the right two red amaryllis raise their proud heads.

Remarks
This kind of composition can only be done by a specialist. However, an amateur given the same materials could construct a similar, but less elaborate arrangement.

The romantic setting

A bouquet of roses in the middle of a round, sophisticated dinner table: lace cloth, with Sèvres porcelain and silver-gilt cutlery. Green velvet ribbons to match the hangings, radiate from the foot of the arrangement.

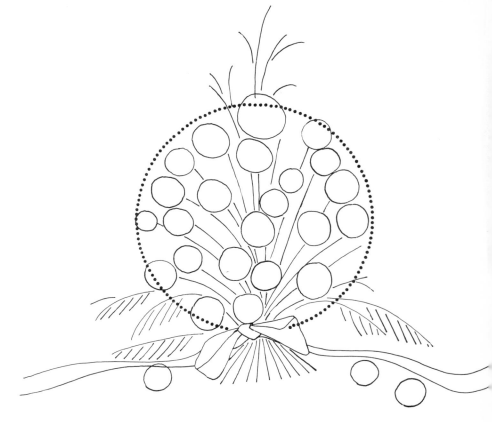

Composition
Mexican aquilegia
Wild oats
Tea roses

Method
Make the arrangement in the hand. The flowers should be gathered together one by one and put round the rose which is the most open. Bind with a green velvet ribbon about 5 inches from the end.

Level up the stalks and separate them out so as to form a cone on which the bouquet stands.

Put some bright pink aquilegias on the ribbons picking up the colour of linen and plates, and a rose knotted with loops of velvet ribbon at each end.

Remarks
Use only garden roses, as they last better. In order that they remain fresh throughout the meal plunge them in water up to the flower heads for several hours before using them.

As you make the bouquet, twist some damp moss between the stems.

When the bouquet is finished, immerse the head quickly in a bowl of cool water and allow to drain.

Once in place, spray very lightly all over the surface.

Variants
Bright red roses on a plain white cloth
White roses on a blue or red cloth

Modern table

This arrangement is reminiscent of a geometrical, abstract painting. The horizontal mass of short-stemmed flowers in monochrome groups, contrasts with the linear effect of the taller flowers. The place settings are neutral in colour, modern in keeping with this austere composition.

Container
Three crystal bowls of different heights by Alvar Aalto

Composition
Garlic flowers (1)
White campanulas (2)
Miniature dahlias (3)
Wallflowers (4)
Ixias (5)
Tiger lilies (6)
Lilies-of-the-valley (7)
Forget-me-nots (8)
Tulips (9)

Method
Set the bowls in the middle of the table to form an ellipse if the table is oval, and a circle if it is round.

Group the flowers into bunches of the same type and cut the stalks to the right lengths. Start with the shallow bowl (lilies-of-the-valley, tulips and tiger lily). Put the mauve ixias in the tallest vase.

Arrange vertically and at different heights some garlic flowers and tiger lilies.

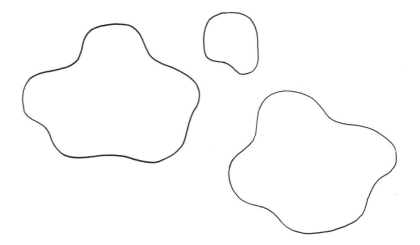

Remarks
Decide in advance how you will arrange the blocks of colour, trying to avoid a too careful symmetry in separating the colours.

Variants
Using the same method, the play of line and colour and choice of flowers is infinite: nasturtiums, primroses, narcissi, iris, tulips, agapanthas, antirrhinums and so on.

146

Flowers and shells

This combination can be used in a number of different ways. This one has an exotic style: hot-house flowers and shells from the South Seas. It brings life to a simple, elegant table setting – embroidered cloth, plain dinner plates and classic glass.

The arrangement of the composition conceals the foundation, a metal tray with a low rim, half filled with water to give enough humidity to keep the flowers fresh for a few hours.

Composition
Acorus
Amaryllis
Caladium
Gloriosa
Orchids
Coral and several shells

Method
Place a pinholder in the centre of the tray and attach two stems of orchids and some acorus to make the centre of the design.

Group the coral and shells round it, leaving small spaces between them. Fill these spaces with leaves and flowers (acorus and gloriosas). Two amaryllis put into the lower edge curve over on to the cloth; this vivid touch of red is balanced by the dark green of a caladium leaf.

Distribute the shells so as to balance the whole, arranging the large shapes alternately with the slender cones dispersed around the outer edge.

Remarks
The speckled cones pick up the colours of the orchids, while cockle shells contrast with the amaryllis. Yellow and red, the flowers blend with the tones of the shells.

Variants
The orchids may be replaced with strelitzias and the amaryllis with anthuriums.

148

Easter

For Easter the table should be decorated with all the Spring flowers. This appealing design is made with Spring blooms, bunched in clusters. Coloured eggs are mingled with the flowers to remind us of Easter. A plain cloth, grass green perhaps, and simple plates with a white ground are best. Simplicity, gaiety, these express the mood.

This composition is easy to make. It is arranged on a simple basket tray, decorated with natural moss.

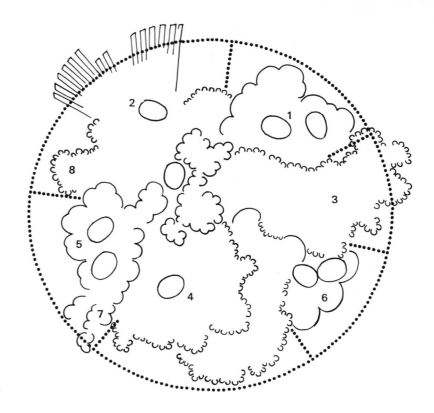

Composition

Gerberas (1)

Ixias (2)

Mauve lilac (3)

Blue forget-me-nots (4)

White daisies (5)

Yellow pansies (6)

Apple blossom (7)

Caladium leaves (8)

Method

The flowers should be prepared beforehand in clusters of equal size.

Put each group on a bed of moss, the strong colours alternating with the pastel colours. For instance, do not put the gerberas next to the yellow pansies; put some mauve lilac between.

In each cluster there are some eggs dyed to match the flowers.

Remarks

The arrangement should not be too symmetrical; bring forward a piece of lilac, apple blossom and some ixias to break the line. This arrangement should look casual; if it is too regular it looks like a park flower-bed.

Variants

All the spring flowers can be used: primroses, crocus, narcissi, lilies-of-the-valley, daffodils, violets, ranunculus.

Alternatively, it is possible to make the centre taller by adding sprigs of apple blossom, syringa, or cherry. They should not be too tall so that they irritate the guests seated opposite each other; an important point to be remembered when making a table centre. At other times of the year, the eggs could be replaced by fruit.

150

The banquet

The tradition of the formal banquet has here been revived in an authentic 17th-century room in the Château of F. The painted ceiling, carved panelling and tapestries are all in the French style of the period. The table is sumptuously laid, recalling the lavishness of the past: white damask cloth, painted porcelain and antique silver. The flower decoration is luxuriant and exotic.

Here, a tropical garden is the inspiration for Jacques Bédat's design. The shaded pinks and greens of the colour scheme blend with the soft tones of the room. The central motif stretches along one third of the table: orchids, the African China rose, poinsettia, pink tulips, pineapple plants and flowering eucalyptus.

There are two made up palm trees, the tops of cycas leaves, and their trunks made from a chain of pineapple fruits. There are two round floral motifs at the ends of the table.

The lighting enhances this beautiful table; hanging from the ceiling is a wonderful crystal and ormolu chandelier which illuminates the whole room. Each place is adorned by a candle in a pineapple. The candles alternate in green and pink, picking up the main colours. Their soft light is supplemented by the twinkling of tiny pink and green electric bulbs concealed in the flowers. (In the foreground the light from within falls on a tulip so that it seems transparent.)

Such a scheme is too ambitious for the amateur. To be successful it needs the skill and taste of a specialist – and the superb setting. But it may still suggest some ideas.

Remarks

The motifs are designed to follow the basic rule: that the height must not block the view of the guests.

This is the plan usually adopted for large receptions. The buffet is generally put at the end, or in a corner of a room, as it is less formal than a dining table. Also, as everything is prepared in advance the serving of the food is made much easier.

The flower arrangement should be imposing and preferably tall. If it is too broad it will get in the way of the dishes set out on the table, and annoy both guests and waiters.

Choose a decorative theme suitable for the occasion or a seasonal subject. In autumn, for instance, a hunting or a woodland theme would be suitable. Plan the colour scheme; it could be brilliant with saffron-yellow linen, pewter plates and groups of fruit, flowers and russet foliage, with some pheasant feathers to accentuate the theme.

Tall pyramids of fruit and vegetables are reminiscent of 18th-century buffets. They should be accompanied with splendid silver and candelabra festooned with mixed foliage and bay leaves. If the buffet table is very long, two pyramids can be placed at either end to complete the design. Improvise with simple materials: a round cabbage, its leaves heavily veined, is arranged on the top of a green glass candlestick. This would make an original and unpretentious decoration for a young party.

Candelabras festooned with ivy, foliage, flowers and fruit form not only a point of light, but they also break the monotony of piles of plates, cutlery and glass. Also candles give a soft light, becoming to both flowers and guests. We would choose white candles so as not to add a discordant note to a brilliantly coloured decoration.

This pyramid of fruit, flowers and vegetables, is inspired by the sumptuous still lifes which were fashionable in the 17th and 18th centuries. Similar arrangements are still used to decorate buffets on grand occasions at Versailles and the Royal Palaces. Although designed for a formal setting, this pyramid would fit perfectly in a humbler background at a country reception, with simple china, pewter dishes and perhaps with some old dark green glass.

Composition

Fruit: Pineapples, avocado pears, cherries, aubergine, strawberries, limes (wild lemons), lichees, coconuts, peaches, apples, black grapes
Vegetables: Artichokes, asparagus, aubergine, cabbage, cucumbers, shallots, fennel, beans, Moroccan beans, melons, peas, pimentos, peppers, radishes, tomatoes, morel mushrooms
Flowers and foliage: Judas tree, spirea, viburnum, chlorophytum, caladium leaves

Method

All these materials are arranged on a number of wooden or basket work trays piled one on top of the other with a netting mould between each one.

Make a firm mould of netting for each tray, and a cone shaped one for the top one. Cover it with natural moss.

Put some of the fruit and vegetables on each tray mixing the colours. Arrange the strawberries in the hollow of single cabbage leaf.

Fix the heavy fruit and vegetables, artichokes, apples, fennel, with wire on the cone.

Using a finer wire, make a ring to support the lighter fruit such as the limes and lichees. Attach this ring to the cone.

Put the pineapple – pierced with a bamboo stick – on top of the pyramid.

Here and there (down the whole length of the pyramid) put in branches of viburnum, Judas tree, and spirea and some of the caladium and chlorophytum leaves. Several of the smaller branches should jut out, and from these dangle bunches of cherries like ornaments on a Christmas tree.

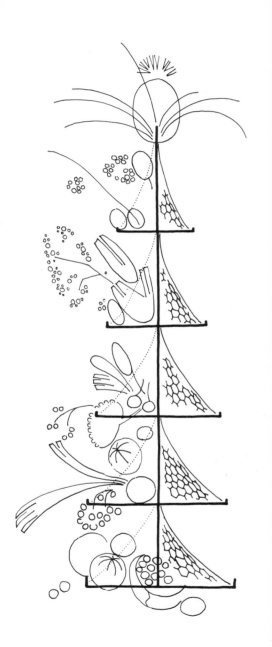

Autumn still-life

In this arrangement the dying splendour of forest, garden and orchard combine with a hunting theme. The brown furry coat of a hare, and the pheasant's plumes nestle into the golden leaves, the last flowers and ripening fruit. A bright saffron cloth completes this warm and rich design. The servers are in the style of the 15th century, copied from miniatures. The pheasant has been drawn and its feathers re-arranged. The décor of foliage, fruit and flowers and corn is repeated on the candelabras.

Composition
Sunflowers
Korean chrysanthemums
Branches of cotoneaster salicifolia
Apples
One hare
Two pheasants

Method
Beside a garnished turbot on a silver dish, the composition is built up on a tiered frame. Fix some wire netting over each tier and cover with natural damp moss. This wire must be firmly constructed, and be strong enough to carry the weight.

Start with the game: attach the hare by its back legs and the pheasants by their heads.

Push the various flowers and foliage into the moss with the sunflowers and a branch of cotoneaster at the top, so that they show up well.

The Korean chrysanthemums are put in groups so as to accentuate their colours. Add flowers, foliage, and fruit alternately. Some of the flowers and branches should jut out from the centre to give a light appearance.

Make a composition at the base like a beautiful still life consisting of apples, sunflowers, chrysanthemums with a branch of cotoneaster lying on the cloth.

Variants
A smaller composition, easier for an amateur, can be made with similar materials and by reducing the height. It is, of course, less spectacular, but no less attractive.

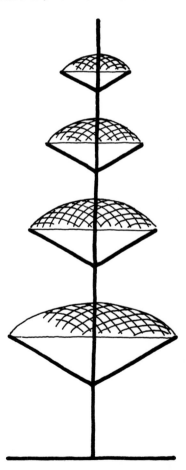

Exotic décor

Sea, sun and luxuriant vegetation – an image of paradise, of light and heat was the inspiration for this buffet for a party held in Paris one dull December day. The tropical atmosphere is produced not only by the choice of plants – palm, exotic fruits and vegetables, but also by the colours, the ultramarine of the linen, brilliant green of the banana leaves and the orange coloured fruits. In the background, a bunch of bananas hanging on the lattice of a window adds to the exotic atmosphere.

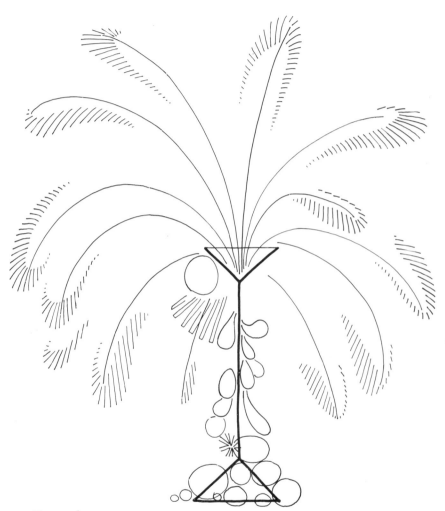

Composition
A small palm
Pineapples
Artichokes
Avocado pears
Pomegranates
Two water melons

Method
Fix the trunk of the palm solidly on a flat, heavy support, an umbrella stand for example. Absolute stability must be ensured from the start. Start the decoration at the bottom of the palm trunk. Wire the artichokes, aubergines and avocados and hang them all down the trunk. The trunk should not be visible. Hang a large water melon in the centre of the palm, half hidden in the branches.

Pile up the remaining fruit and vegetables to conceal the tray at the base.

Put in the banana leaves on either side so that they lie flat on the cloth and so complete the arrangement.

Remarks
The food chosen for the buffet should suit the décor. The arrangement would not look suitable with game, or elaborately decorated or sophisticated Parisian dishes; a simple menu including iced punch, fresh fruit and conserves would be better. Do not use elaborate silver, it would be out of place.

Buffet for young people

One evening one has to improvise. There is to be an impromptu party with no time to make a flower decoration and, in any case, flowers in winter are expensive. Here is an amusing and very decorative idea, costing very little, for decorating a table or sideboard: a cabbage on a stand. It looks a little sad, perched so high, so to cheer it up put a tiny bunch of yellow chrysanthemums nestling between the leaves. This small splash of colour gives a lively effect.

Container
A tinted glass candlestick by the Finnish designer, Oivo Troïkka, surmounted by a large moveable socket.

Choose a well rounded cabbage. This is an ordinary cabbage, but there are also decorative varieties with large green and pink leaves.

Perhaps, instead of green cabbage, find a red one and decorate it with red flowers, anemones for instance. The effect is exciting.

Variants
Here is another suggestion: the cabbage is hollowed out like a chalice and filled with flowers (in this case, anemones). Separate the other leaves carefully and insert them between the erect heads of the flowers. Alternate the colours and so avoid a uniform effect. Leave some gaps so that the flowers stand out in relief.

Raise a few of the flower heads, they should stand out above the design.

Barbecue

An arrangement of aromatic herbs stands in the chimney corner appealing to both sight and smell. All the sweet smelling spices and herbs which flavour the cooking are close at hand. The guests can pluck a bay leaf, a sprig of rosemary or a branch of tarragon as they will. The large rhubarb leaves can be used to 'fan' the fire.

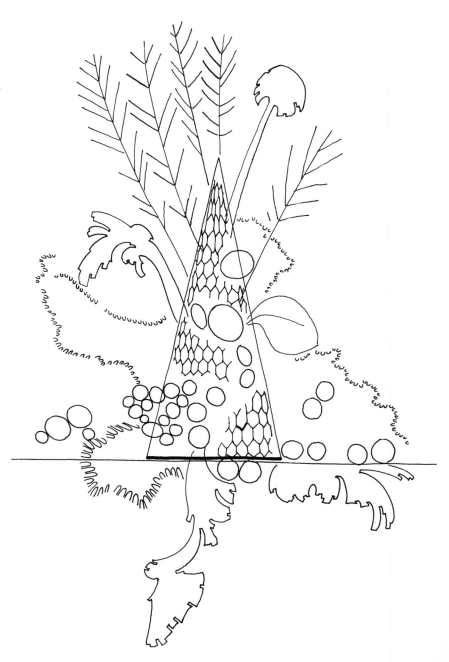

Composition

Garlic	Onions
Celery	Parsley
Spring onions	Pimento
Lemons	Rosemary
Cress	Sage
Tarragon	Thyme
Bay	Tomatoes

Method

Make a wire cone; fill it with natural or synthetic moss, and cover it with natural moss. Fix this cone on a firm wooden base.

Arrange the herbs into small bunches, and bind them with wire leaving a loop which will be used to hang them on the cone. Work from the bottom upwards. Finish the top with a few branches of bay.

Put a large rhubarb leaf, a bunch of thyme, two lemons, tomatoes and a stick of celery around the base, showing their contrasting colours and shapes to advantage. The finished arrangement should look like a still life, rather casual, and not too stiff.

162

Harvest Festival

A Harvest Festival is the thanksgiving service held every autumn in the church of England. The church is decorated with fruit, flowers, foliage and vegetables as thanksgiving for the fruits of the earth. This composition by Mrs. Sheila Macqueen was designed for this festival.

Warm tones recall the splendour of garden and woods and the past generosity of nature. Some exotic flowers have been introduced to enhance the charm of the rest.

Container
Marble bowl on a stand

Composition

Flowers:	Foliage:
Amaranthus	Curly cabbage
Gerberas	Croton
Gladioli	Mahonia
Hippeastrum	Golden privet
Hydrangea	
Magnolia	Fruit:
Pelargonium	Pineapples
Baccara roses	Quinces
Polyanthus roses	Courgettes (baby marrows)
Saxifrage	Pomegranates
Stone-crop	White grapes

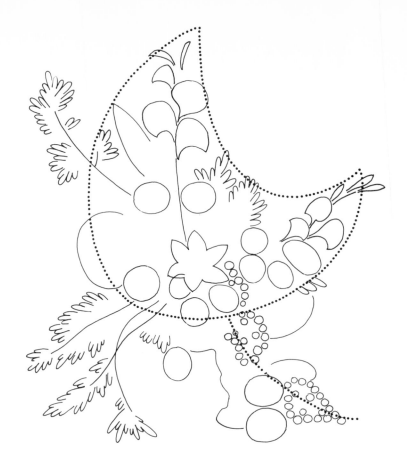

The whole arrangement forms an asymmetrical triangle. Group all the bright flowers at the centre: red roses, gerberas, with a magnificent red hippeastrum accentuating the focal point. Fill the spaces alternately with flowers, fruit and foliage, contrasting a pineapple's rough skin with a delicate rose. A downy yellow quince is hidden beneath a pale hydrangea, while amaranthus cascades to the foot of the arrangement, like the bunch of grapes. This 'still life' is completed by fruit placed at the foot of the vase.

Method
The flowers are held by a large pinholder and netting moulded to fit the vase. Put in a branch of privet and one gladiolus in the middle, at a height, roughly one and a half times that of the bowl. The line at the base, curving slightly to the right, is made by a gladiolus and one or two branches of privet.

Remarks
This kind of arrangement would also suit a country reception, or a young people's buffet. There should be no cloth: the polished wood of an old table is best for this country theme. The accessories here are pewter; but simple pottery with large coloured glasses would be no less charming.

Buffet party in England

See composition 'Easter' p.150 (variant)

It is not always easy to lay hands on the rare and exotic fruits and flowers of the specialists. But a well-stocked garden is an inexhaustible source of material. Picked fresh the fruit still keeps its velvet down, and the flowers their fresh brilliance. And for an evening party let the plants have an airing from their boring hot-house! Mrs. Ella Forrester has created this simple and pleasant arrangement for a buffet. It is an excellent example of the use of material that is readily available.

Container
A tiered compote dish

Composition

Flowers and leaves:	*Fruit and vegetables:*
Summer jasmine	Apricots
Hot-house carnations	Aubergines
Baccara roses	Green figs
Apricot roses 'Woburn Abbey'	Apples
Skimmia japonica	Black and white grapes
Tellima grandiflora	

Method
The fruit and vegetables are arranged first on the lower tier with a bunch of black grapes hanging over the edge. At the back 'Woburn Abbey' roses, inserted in damp moss, show their heads. The flowers and foliage at the top should be arranged separately in a bowl filled with water. This is placed on the top tier. Add several carnations with long stalks and alternate them with Baccara roses and jasmine. They spread out fanwise at the very top.

The decorations begin at the doorway; a frame of foliage, dried flowers and fruit mingled with cockades of ribbon makes a cheerful decoration to the most commonplace door. An overture of welcome for our friends.

Composition

Lemons	Cedar, pine and fir branches
Oranges	Holly
Apples	Clematis seeds
Grapes	Ears of corn
Pine and fir cones	Dried thistles

Other materials

Plywood
Cardboard
Light wire netting
Nails, steel wire and S – hooks

Method

Prepare a plywood frame to fit the exterior measurements of the door and about 2¾ in. wide. Cover with wire netting fixed with tin-tacks to the back. A strip of cardboard nailed or screwed on the back will cover the rough surface and prevent its scratching the wall.

The frame, placed in position, is fixed to the casing of the door. Arrange fruit, dried flowers and pine cones in clusters securing the ends with wire. Tie the feathery clematis seeds into small bunches and powder with artificial snow. Hang the different things on the wire netting with hooks.

Fill in the gaps with branches of cedar, pine, fir or holly and here and there insert a few ears of corn and cockades of red ribbon.

Remarks

Use both natural and artificial fruit. The latter are lighter, more durable, and less tempting to the guests!

Christmas garlands

The garland and the wreath are undoubtedly among the oldest decorative designs. Greeks and Romans used them for temples and houses on feast days. There are many traces in the wall paintings of Pompeii. But this kind of decoration cannot be improvised. It takes time and patience and should be carefully prepared. There are two possible methods:

Vertical garland
Cut a strip of wire netting to the shape and dimensions required ending in a point at one end.

Group together the cones, fruits and small branches in separate bunches tied with wire. Hang them with S-hooks to the wire support.

Remarks
Start at the top with the largest things, graduating the rest down to the bottom.

Pliant garland
to festoon a fireplace, door or window. Tie each bunch with raffia, then form a plait of the desired length inserting fruit, foliage, pine cones, ears of corn and so on. When the plait is finished, fill the gaps with sprigs of holly, pine or fir.

Artificial snow can be powdered on from a pressurized container.

Composition
On the left: Pine or fir cones, laurel leaves, ears of corn and artificial grapes
On the right: Aucuba, fir, cones and apples

Blackamoor flower holder

Of Venetian origin, these blackamoor flower holders in painted and gilded wood were very popular in the 18th century.

This one stands on an octagonal pedestal bearing in his
hand a tray which formerly held a torch. Mme Camilla
Malvasia has substituted for this a spray of fruits, ears of
corn and foliage, reminiscent of the traditional offerings of
the Three Kings.

Composition
Ears of corn
Apples
Grapes
Branches of cedar
Pine and juniper
Common and variegated ivy

Method
Fill a low bowl with synthetic moss and surround it with wire.
Fix this flower holder securely to the tray with wire.

The bunches of grapes are attached with strong wire. The
apples are mounted on a small stick and stuck into the moss.

Add some ears of corn, arranged in clusters, and some pine,
cedar and juniper branches. The ivy trails and falls in a light
cascade down the braided tunic of the blackamoor.

Leathley Hall

A floral wreath hangs on the door and welcomes the guests to the party. Mr. George Smith has created this one in the fine setting of Leathley Hall. Flowers, fruit, foliage and berries recall the splendid faïence reliefs of the 16th century, executed in the Della Robbia studios in Florence. A deep Christmas red in the form of a velvet ribbon twines through the motif, falling in two long ends.

Composition
Flowers: Christmas roses
Fruit and vegetables: Lemons, ears of maize, green and red pimento, apples, grapes (natural or artificial)
Foliage and berries: Holly, laurel, pine, fir and rowan

Method
Make or buy a wire framework; two circles linked together by radiating spokes. Cover with foliage: holly, pine and fir (the small branches about 6 inches long can be intertwined or attached with wire). First cover the left half, then the right, starting again from the same point.

Hang fruits and vegetables with an S-hook or wire and set a large orange on the top.

Christmas roses are very delicate, and will barely last the evening, so wrap the stems in damp moss (these flowers do not take kindly to synthetic moss).

171

A romantic Christmas

Is it so unusual to celebrate the winter season with spring flowers? Holly, mistletoe and the fir tree are traditional in Europe. But there is no reason why we should not depart from convention now that the growers can offer lilac, daffodils and exotic flowers, even in the depth of winter.

Jacques Bédat illustrates an idea for this kind of arrangement.

Container
A low circular bowl about 12 inches in diameter

Composition

Agapanthus	Narcissi
Anemones	Marguerites
Korean chrysanthemums	Prunus
Iris	Christmas roses
Lilac	Dwarf tulips
Daffodils	A spray of blackthorn

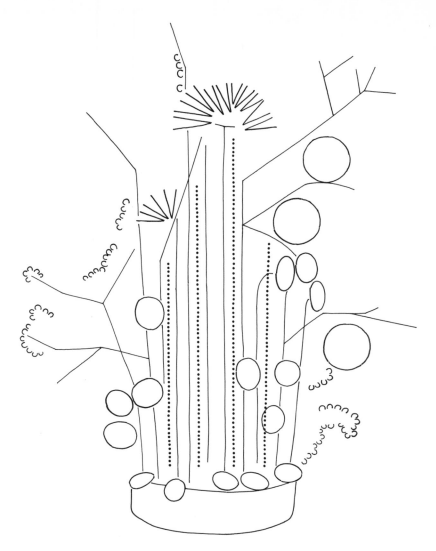

Method
Choose a curving blackthorn branch, strip all twigs and thorns from the lower part and cut the end. Spray with gold paint.

Fill the bowl with synthetic moss and press down lightly. Put in the short stemmed flowers: marguerites, chrysanthemums, Christmas roses and prunus so as to cover the whole surface.

In the centre place the blackthorn, a branch of prunus, the tallest agapanthus, and, parallel to it, a second but shorter agapanthus.

Arrange the other flowers: the lilacs on the right spreading outwards and above them a cluster of narcissi. Fill in the base, both front and back with anemones, daffodils, Christmas roses and dwarf tulips.

Near the gilded branch, insert two irises and a full blown daffodil. Finally, hang three yellow silk Japanese balls on the branch of thorn. They fit into the space on the right and hang swinging gently.

Remark
This arrangement is entirely perpendicular and has no focal point.

The German tradition

Here are a few pretty, but simple ideas suggested by German and Scandinavian folklore. They are intended primarily for people living in the country who like to use natural material: dried flowers, pine cones, berries, fir and holly branches gathered at random whilst out walking.

Fruit, flowers, candles
Lemons, apples, oranges, grapes are placed together in an antique plate. Add some pine cones and branches of blue cedar. A taller branch with a graceful curve stands in the middle. Christmas roses in flower or bud, two white balls, and three candles complete the arrangement.

Green fir and red apples
A cone of wire netting is covered with small fir branches. The ornament: three rows of gilded nuts suspended on wire. Stand the cone upright in a basket and surround it by a circle of red apples each stuck with a candle. Use the same apple-candlestick design at the top of the tree.

An artificial orange tree
A large wire netting ball is fixed to the top of a stake which is fixed a flower pot. Cover the surface with sprigs of holly woven into the mesh. Using wire or hooks, hang the oranges, nuts, small mushrooms, dried flowers etc., on the ball. Round pebbles disguise the base.

Pyramids of nuts and pine cones
This design demands a lot of patience, but children will prove eager helpers. You will need: pine cones, fir cones, and nuts. Wire them and attach them to a netting frame. Place the heavier things at the base so that they help to balance the pyramid. Fill the spaces with dried flowers, keeping to the same neutral tones. The pyramid stands in a flower pot, on a circlet of fir branches.

174

Simple arrangement to celebrate a birth

The great Flemish or Italian primitives, when painting a Nativity, always placed a wreath of symbolic flowers at the Virgin's side. But it is not necessary to use the traditional lily, rose or carnation. This light, elegant bouquet expresses fresh innocence in white and pastel shades. Very vivid colours have been deliberately omitted.

Container
A straight-sided vase covered with pale pink corrugated paper

Composition

Agapanthus	Christmas roses
Anemones	Tulips
Antirrhinum	Foliage of golden thuya

Method
Put a spiked flower holder at the bottom of the vase.

A little back from the centre insert the agapanthus and antirrhinums (the height of the stems being three times the height of the vase). The head of agapanthus stands clear, dominating the arrangement. Put in the front a cluster of anemones, and on the left one tulip, slightly slanting, and another behind it. Tuck in two Christmas roses near the rim of the vase, with their heads leaning over the edge (Christmas roses have very short stems).

Add some branches of golden thuya which give a rich effect. Spread out the branches on the left, and angle the longer branch on the right sharply downwards. This slanting line counterbalances the vertical lines of the flowers in the centre.

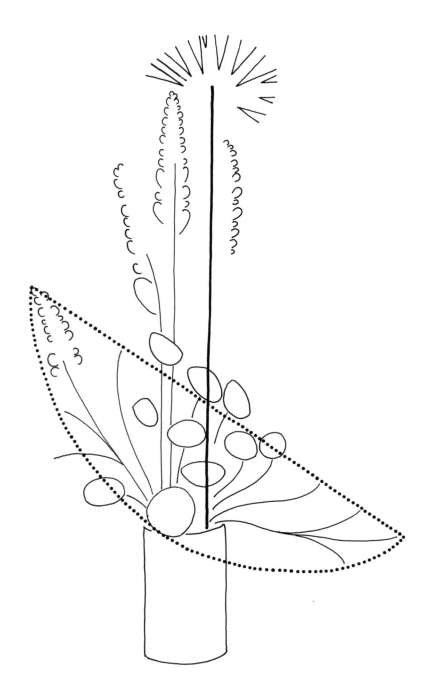

176

Christening

The cabbage: from this commonplace object, Jacques Bédat
has made a very imaginative arrangement. It makes a delight-
ful decoration for a christening. It also has the advantage of
being easy to make.

Container
A low circular bowl about 12 inches across

Composition
A large rounded curly cabbage – preferably the ornamental kind
White anemones with mauve centres
Prunus
Pink tulips

Method
Fill the bowl with synthetic moss, and press it down lightly.
Strip the leaves from the cabbage and place the larger ones
against the outer edge of the bowl. Continue towards the
centre adding leaves, anemones and tulips in turn. Keep to
the fat, round shape of a cabbage.

In the centre put in a few prunus branches with, here and
there, some long tulip leaves, folded like the loops of ribbon.
This detail is not essential and as it gives a more artificial note
to the arrangement it may be omitted.

Variants
Carefully hollow out the heart of the cabbage, and fill this
space with a fine full blown rose.

A cabbage, placed in a low bowl is surrounded by a circlet
of flowers.

Another way is to set cherry branches all round: the effect
very gay and springlike.

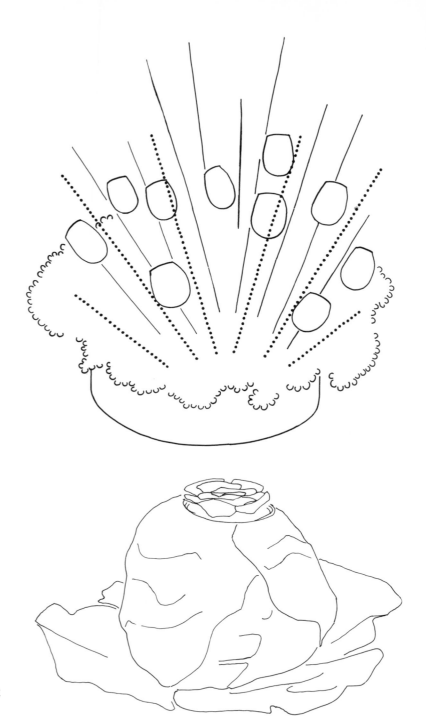

178

Wedding

Jacques Bédat here departs from the traditional 'wedding basket'. He was inspired by a Persian miniature to create this centre-piece for a wedding breakfast. It is built on a solid wire frame, and the curving side branches are attached to a rigid central stem. This frame is fixed into a bowl filled with synthetic, and damp natural moss.

Composition
White amaryllis
White lilac
Antirrhinums
Bunches of daisies
Prunus
Magnolia leaves

Method
At each intersection of the branches and the stem, attach a piece of synthetic moss with wire. This is necessary to keep the flowers fresh.

'Dress' the framework – the branches with prunus in bud, and the central stem with antirrhinums. Fasten them here and there with green wire. Put a small piece of lilac at the top of each branch.

At the three points of intersection, stick into the clumps of moss an amaryllis (in the centre) and two bunches of daisies, surrounded by magnolia leaves. Note that the upper bunch is framed by four smaller ones.

At the top, place a tall stem of wallflower so that its upright line is clearly defined. At the foot, group three amaryllis with two sloping stems of wallflowers on either side. Magnolia leaves arranged in a ring hide the base.

Golden wedding

This handsome, colourful arrangement rises like a flame from the centre of the sideboard. Fifty years of marriage is an occasion to celebrate. This elaborate design demands considerable experience in the art of flower arrangement. The basic shape is an isosceles triangle.

Container
A cut glass urn-shaped vase with ormolu mount

Composition

Korean chrysanthemums	Daffodils
Freesias	Tiger lilies
Gerberas	Antirrhinums

Method
Put some wire netting into the vase. The focal point of the design is nearly central at the back of the vase.

At this point, put in the tall flowers which form the axis of the arrangement. We have chosen two antirrhinums as their slender flowers make the apex of the design. Strip off the bottom leaves.

Make the lower line with the pliant flowers: freesias, daffodils, arranged on either side of the axis and towards the front, falling naturally. Stiffness would destroy the general line.

Build up the arrangement round this structure keeping its pyramid shape. Alternate the colours to maintain a balanced whole. A group of tiger lilies at the base, make a colourful centre of interest.

Remarks
Avoid heavy-looking flowers with too open blooms. The effect is made by the warm shades of the same colour range.

182

FIELD, WOODLAND AND GARDEN FLOWERS

Meadows in spring, gardens in summer and the woods in autumn, offer many possibilities to the flower lover. Scarlet pimpernel, sorrel and wild carrot flourish on the banks; orchids, scabious and daisies adorn the fields; the hawthorn and honeysuckle abound in the hedges, whilst the bullrush, queen of the meadow, haunts the marsh.

The wide variety of natural flowers provide a wealth of material for country-house arrangements. Simplicity and spontaneity are the keynote. Avoid sophistication; the elaborate vase and an exaggerated effect. Country flowers are not suited to the same treatment as a hot-house or exotic plant.

Shrub or fruit tree branches may be used at all seasons. If in flower they should be cut in bud or they will drop too quickly. In summer, coloured berries must not be too ripe. In winter, the blackthorn or the mossy branch of an old tree have great charm with their clear, strong, curves. Cut cleanly with a pruning knife. Do not mutilate young trees with their promise of the future.

Finland

An armful of flowers, gathered at random during a country walk, is arranged casually.

Composition

Wild carrot leaves	Larkspur
Ivy	Grasses
Marguerites	

Method

The flowers arrange themselves without effort. It will be enough to loosen, here and there, a hidden flower head, to relieve the congestion.

Its charm lies in the evocation of a flowery meadow at the beginning of June – a miracle of nature. Nothing more is needed.

Field flowers

Stoneware vases and simple flowers
Which is the complement of the other? It is difficult to separate the two elements in these compositions by Robert Deblander:

pimpinella
cladium leaves
a fine heracleum leaf

The slender line of the stalks and leaves contrast with the compact mass of a heracleum leaf set towards the back. There is a hint of poetry in the tiny flowering branch.

The countryside in miniature
A big bunch of wild flowers:
Small-flowered arnicas
Wild carrots
Thistles
Sorrel
and a large sunflower are placed together in a glazed earthenware pitcher.

First put in the big stems, sorrel, wild carrots and the sunflower. Put in a large bunch of the smaller flowers, they will help to hold up the remaining grasses.

Garden flowers

The climbing *cobaea scandens,* a native of Mexico, has large bell-shaped flowers. This arrangement, created in England by Mrs. Jocelyn Steward, shows to advantage the corolla and calyx in varying stages of opening. Beautiful hosta leaves form a greenish frame for these flowers. Three sharp croton leaves, like arrows in the background, outline the composition. This simple arrangement is a good example of balance and proportion.

Two marguerites and some marigolds lean on the rim of a soft-toned rough vase. The shadow of the tall grasses casts no shade over the flowers. Note the proportion and balance of line and volume, and the important role of the stems, as in Japanese arrangements.

A pine branch spreads its twisting arms over a stoneware vase, simple as a rock. The line recalls certain Japanese compositions of the *nage-ire* style, but here there is no symbolism.

The charm of the flower, the decorative simplicity of the whole and the art of the photographer are here combined. From the tip of the roots to the topmost bud, nothing interferes with the vibrant line of this lily-of-the-valley. The same results can be obtained from various bulbous plants, especially hyacinths.

Red hawthorn and mauve lilac: the freshness, the colour and scent of early spring. The delicate, well defined foliage, lightens the thick mass formed by the clusters of flowers. The only artificial note in this beautiful amateur arrangement (created in the United States), is the flowering branch inside the vase. It is certainly a decorative but ephemeral for the flowers wither quickly in water. *Note* the crossing of the stems leaning against the side of the vase – this steadies the arrangement in the vase.

192

Anemones, hyacinths, daffodils and ranunculus; here is a whole spring litany in a stemmed glass. Mr. Tom Wier arranged these freshly gathered flowers simply in harmonizing colours. The pale pink rather insipid, hyacinth is enlivened by the red anemone. These spring flowers make charming arrangements. This type of arrangement has inspired several painters.

Simple flowers, hawthorn, cineraria, cotoneaster, hyacinths, viburnum and different leaves, a subdued palette of restrained colours. Forceful shapes and violent colour are excluded from this arrangement. The flowers are built up in stages from the broad base. The container: a glass bowl on a pedestal. A flower holder in the bottom ensures stability.

193

Old fashioned roses, tea roses, and miniature roses mingle with brilliant red polyanthus roses. Becoming increasingly rare, these old varieties have incomparable charm; nothing is so sweet as their perfume...

They recall the gardens of the First Empire and the folios of Redouté. All together in a jardinière, they are mutually enhanced. The soft tone of the tea roses forms a delicate centre to this glowing arrangement.

DRIED FLOWERS

Dried flowers are prepared in the summer when they are in full bloom, and are precious in winter when other flowers are scarce and expensive. They make as decorative arrangements as the fresh ones, and they can be kept for several years as well.

The drying process is easy, but methods differ for various plants.

Fresh air

Achillea, allium, acroclinium, arctotis, astilbe, thistles, delphinium, dipsacus, eryngium, eulalia, gynerium, heracleum, hortensia, everlasting flowers, lagurus, honesty, physalis, statice and zinnia.

Cut the flowers just before they are fully open: Strip the leaves and hang them upside down without constricting them. Some kinds (lagurus and grasses) dry better upright and should be placed in bottles. Their stems are less stiff than those that are dried hanging and they are useful for decorations needing pliant curves.

The drying process will be more rapid in a warm, airy, and if possible, dark room. Allow two or three weeks.

Light as a Japanese sunshade, these strange Australian anemones are accompanied by fine plumes of stipa and the downy spears of lagurus ovatus.

Glycerine water
All evergreen leaves; aucuba, camellia, eucalyptus, ivy, magnolia and mahonia.
Prepare equal parts of a solution of water and glycerine. Submerge the stems approximately 4 to 5 inches. If the stem is woody, crush or slice the end. Leave to soak from two to four weeks, checking the level of the liquid from time to time. The leaves will take on a fine patina which will not change even if used with fresh flowers in water.

Borax
Clematis, cosmos, everlasting flowers, iris, gladiolus, pansy, rose and carnation. This process has the advantage of preserving the colour of the flowers. Place the flowers in a box containing borax, head downwards on the powder. Every flower must be isolated from its neighbour. Cover with a fairly thick layer of borax and place the box in a warm and dry place. Leave for about a week, but no longer, as they may disintegrate.

Allium albopilosum (garlic flower)
Cut before the flower is fully mature. If too ripe the seeds will drop. Place the stem upright into a bottle and leave to dry

Heracleum (giant hog weed)
The flower must be picked at the end of the summer after it is completely dried

Pressing

Ferns, autumn leaves (oak, maple, beech, hazel, chestnut) should be placed between pages of a newspaper. Press firmly, under heavy books for example, and leave for three to four weeks.

Lunaria (honesty)

Wait until the seeds are ripe, that is when the pods split. Hang upside down.

Lagurus ovatus (hare's tail)

Pick when in flower and dry in a bottle with the head outside.

Period arrangement

Like a dress of moonbeams, or of glittering gauze, radiant as a fairy tale, this bouquet shimmers with sweet fantasy, but it is as decorative as a spray of fresh flowers. The honesty's silver coins are iridescent with reflections like the silver vase, while copper tones add warmth. Spidery plants, umbellifera and grasses make a misty halo. The neutral tones, with no colour accents, blend with the patina of old furniture in a period interior.

Container
A two-handled silver vase

Composition
Allium albopilosum
Thistles
Eryngium
Heracleum
Helichrysum
Lunaria (honesty)
Lagurus ovatus
Various grasses

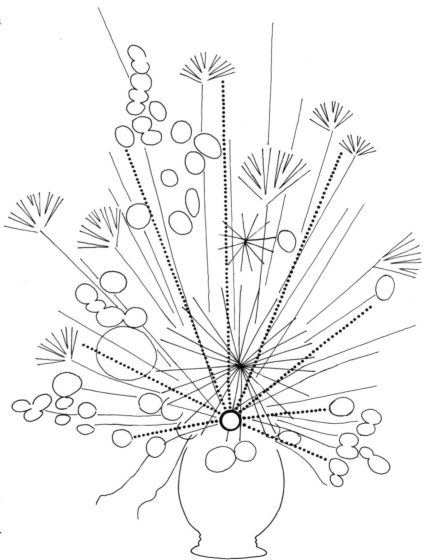

Method
The heavy oval shape recalls the Louis XIV arrangement.

The symmetrically arranged flowers radiate around a focal point, accented by a large head of Heracleum.

Honesty forms the basis of the arrangement. The other flowers make the outline and give balance.

200

The poetry of autumn

This is a very modern arrangement of dried flowers, designed by Jacques Bédat with the flower heads of vegetables, garden flowers, and one or two exotic elements. Its faded tones recall the dying spirit of autumn. In this symphony of greys, there are one or two soft colours: achillea, so aptly called 'plate of gold' and the orange tones of physalis and cotoneaster leaves. The composition is tall, vertical, and rectangular.

Container
Cylindrical terra cotta pot harmonizing with the tones of the arrangement

Composition
Achillea
Datura leaves
Eryngium
Grasses
Helianthus of different sizes
Everlasting flowers
Heads of lettuce and leek
Plantain spears

Method
Fill the container with dry synthetic moss and press it down firmly. It should be very compact to hold the flowers. Put the grasses and lettuce seed heads upright in the moss, and a little to the back to form an airy background for the more solid elements.
Place the three largest leeks in diminishing order in the centre, one at the bottom and towards the front. The smallest should be placed high up, centred on the main axis. Put the datura leaves behind, their ribbed translucency suits the firm roundness of the leek heads. Finish off with achillea, everlasting flowers, plantain and physalis. The composition is light and airy at the top and grows thicker towards the base. Put branches of eryngium along the edge of the vase to form a spiny ruff. To the right cotoneaster branch enlivens the effect without breaking the line. Avoid a rigid effect.

Very modern in conception, this arrangement fits a décor in neutral tones of white, beige or brown. It fits equally well into a country or early style. It should never be placed in an 18th- or 19th-century setting, or anywhere with strong colours.

Spike, flowers and branch extend the soaring line of a stoneware vase rough as bark. All the different parts of the composition are in harmony. It is interesting to see how the stems have been used to make a linear design in the Japanese manner.

Glossary

Acroclinium
African lily   *Agapanthus*
African marigold   *Tagetes erecta*
Amaryllis   *Hippeastrum*
Antirrhinum
Anemone
Apricot   *Prunus armenaica*
Arctotis grandis
Arnica montana
Asparagus officinalis
Aspidistra
Astilbe   *Hoteia japonica*
Aubergine   *Solanum melongena*
Aucuba
Auratum lily   *Lilium auratum*
Avocado   *Persea gratissima*

Beans   *Vicia faba*
Begonia rex
Berberis   *Berberis thunbergii*
Blackcurrent   *Ribes nigrum*
Blue cedar   *Cedrus atlanticus glaucus*
Blue thistle   *Eryngium amethystum*
Box   *Buxus sempervirens arborescens*
Broom   *Genista*
Buddleia Davidi magnifica

Cabbage   *Brassica oleracea*
Cactus
Caladium
Camellia
Campanula   *Campanula pyramidalis*
  Carpathian campanula   *Campanula carpathica*
Candytuft   *Iberis*
Carnation   *Dianthus caryophyllus*
Carrot   *Daucus carota* (root)

Carrot leaf   *Daucus carota*
Cattleya
Caucasian scabious   *Scabiosa caucasica*
  Annual scabious (Pincushion flower)   *Scabiosa atropurpurea*
Celery   *Apium graveolens*
Cherry   *Cerasus*
Chestnut   *Aesculus*
China rose   *Rosa chinensis*
Chinese lantern   *Physalis*
Chives   *Allium schoenoprasum*
Chlorophytum elatum variegatum
Christmas rose   *Helleborus niger*
Chrysanthemum
Clematis
Clerodendrum
Climbing lily   *Gloriosa*
Cobaea scandens
Columbine   *Aquilegia*
Copper beech   *Fagus silvatica atropurpurea*
Coreopsis
Cosmos bipinnatus
Cotoneaster
Cow parsley   *Heracleum*
Crab apple   *Malus pumila*
Crassula falcata
Croton   *Codiaeum variegatum pictum*
Cucumber   *Cucumis sativus*
Cultivated mushroom   *Psalliota*

Dahlia
Day lily (hybrid)   *Hemerocallis (hybrida)*
Double daisy   *Bellis perennis*
Double stock   *Matthiola incana*

Echinops
Elm   *Ulmus campestris*
Eremurus
Eucalyptus
Eulalia
Euphorbia
Everlasting flowers   *Helichrysum bracteatum*

Fennel   *Foeniculum*
Fern   *Filix*
Fig   *Ficus*
Fir   *Abies*
Forget-me-not   *Myosotis alpestris*
Forsythia
Foxglove   *Digitalis*
Freesia
Fritillary   *Fritillaria*

Gaillardia
Garlic   *Allium sativum*
Gladiolus
Globe artichoke   *Cynara scolymus*
Godetia
Gooseberry   *Ribes grossularia*
Grape   *Vitis vinifera*
Grasses   *Gramineae*
Green haricot   *Phaseolus*
Grevillea
Guelder rose   *Viburnum opulus sterilis*
Gypsophila paniculata

Hare's tail   *Lagurus ovatus*
Hawthorn   *Crataegus*
Hazel   *Corylus*
Helenium
Holly   *Ilex aquifolium*

Hollyhock   *Althaea rosea*
Honesty   *Lunaria annua*
Honeysuckle   *Lonicera caprifolium*
Hosta
Hyacinth   *Hyacinthus*
Hydrangea

Iris
Iris Susiana
Ivy   *Hedera helix*
Ixia

Jasmine   *Jasminum*
Jonquil   *Narcissus jonquilla*
Judas tree   *Cercis siliquastrum*
Juniper   *Juniperus*

Korean chrysanthemum   *Chrysanthe-mum koreanum*
Kola nut   *Cola acuminata*

Laburnum
Larch   *Larix*
Larkspur   *Delphinium ajacis*
Laurustinus   *Viburnum tinus*
Lemon   *Citrus limonia*
Lettuce   *Lactuca sativa*
Liatris
Li chi   *Nephelium*
Lilac   *Syringa vulgaris*
Lily of the valley   *Convallaria majalis*
Lime   *Citrus aurantifolia*
Love-lies-bleeding   *Amaranthus caudatus*
Lupin   *Lupinus*
Lychnis coronaria

Madonna lily   *Lilium candidum*
Magnolia
Mahonia
Maize   *Zea mays*
Mallow   *Lavatera*
Maple   *Acer*
Marrow   *Cucurbita pepo*
Melon   *Cucumis melo*
Moss rose   *Rosa centifolia*

Narcissus
Nasturtium   *Tropaeolum*
Nephrolepis
Nidularium

Oak   *Quercus*
Oats   *Avena sativa*
Onion   *Allium cepa*
Orange   *Citrus sinensis*
Orchid   *Orchideae*
Ox-eyed-daisy   *Chrysanthemum leucan-themum*

Pansy   *Viola tricolor*
Parsley   *Petroselinum hortense*
Peach   *Persica*
Peas   *Pisum sativum*
Pearly everlasting flower   *Anaphalis mar-garitacea*
Peony   *Paeonia*
Pepper   *Capsicum annuum*
Peruvian lily   *Alstroemeria*
Philadelphus   *Philadelphus coronarius*
Phlox
Pimpinella
Pineapple   *Ananas sativus*
Pine   *Pinus*
Pinks   *Dianthus plumarius*
Plantain   *Plantago*
Poinsettia
Pomegranate   *Punica granatum*
Poppy   *Papaver*
Primrose   *Primula vulgaris*
Privet   *Ligustrum ovalifolium*
Prunus
Pussy willow   *Salix caprea*
Pyrethrum

Quince   *Cydonia oblonga*

Radish   *Raphanus sativus*
Ranunculus
Raspberry   *Rubus*
Reed mace   *Typha*
Reeds   *Arundo donax (Phragmites)*
Rhubarb   *Rheum*
Rowan   *Sorbus*
Rosemary   *Rosmarinus*

Santolina
Saxifrage   *Saxifraga*
Sea ragwort   *Senecio cineraria*
Sea rushes   *Cladium mariscus*
Sedum spurium
Shallot   *Allium ascalonicum*

Skimmia japonica
Solomon's seal   *Polygonatum*
Spiraea
Stag's horn sumach   *Rhus typhina*
Statice   *Limonium*
Strawberry   *Fragaria*
Strelitzia
Sunflower   *Helianthus annuus*
Sweet bay   *Laurus nobilis*
Sweet flag   *Acorus calamus*
Sweet pea   *Lathyrus odoratus*
Sweet pepper (Pimento)   *Capsicum*
Sweet-scented mignonette *Reseda odorata*
Sweet William   *Dianthus barbatus*

Tamarisk   *Tamarix pentandra*
Tarragon   *Artemisia dracunculus*
Teasel   *Dipsacus*
Tellima grandiflora
Thistle   *Cnicus*
Thuya
Thyme   *Thymus*
Tiger lily   *Lilium tigrinum*
Tigridia
Tobacco flower   *Nicotiana sanderae*
Tomato   *Solanum lycopersicum*
Tulip   *Tulipa*

Viburnum carlesii
Violet   *Viola*

Wallflower   *Cheiranthus*
Wallnut   *Juglans regia*
Water cress   *Nasturtium officinale*
Water grasses   Gynerium
Water melon   *Citrullus vulgaris*
Wayfaring tree   *Viburnum lantana*
Wheat   *Triticum vulgare*
Wild blue salvia   *Salvia pratensis*
Wild hemlock   *Comium maculatum*
Wild mignonette   *Reseda asolaich*
Wild parsley   *Anthriscus sylvestris*
Wild sorrel   *Rumex acetosa*
Wistaria chinensis

Yarrow   *Achillea*
Yellow flag water iris   *Iris pseudacorus*

Zinnia

Acknowledgements

The photographs illustrating this volume were placed at our disposal by:

Bagel, Paris: p. 128 (arrangement: X)

Cyril Bernard, London: p. 166 (arrangement: Ella Forrester)

Ken Brunton Lauder, Galerie Voir, Tonbridge: p.92 (arrangement: Aaronson)

Buzzini, Paris: p. 174 at the top (arrangement: X)

Julia Clements, London: pp. 43, 47, 111 (photographs and arrangements)

Connaissance des Arts, Paris: pp. 137 (photograph: Pascal Hinous), 145 (photograph: Michel Nahmias), 147 (photograph: Hinous)

R. Deblander, Paris: (by kind permission of *Maison Française,* Paris) pp. 188, 190 (vases and arrangements)

Elle, Paris: p. 189 (photograph: Edi Vogt, arrangement: X)

Warren Jepson, Leeds: pp. 117, 171 (arrangements: George W. Smith)

Pierre Joly and Véra Cardot, Paris: p. 204 (vase and arrangement: Jean and Jacqueline Lerat)

Lavinia Press, Copenhagen: pp. 101, 187, 193 (arrangements: X)

Sheila Macqueen, London: pp. 81, 165 (photographs and arrangements)

Camilla Cagli Malvasia, Bologne: pp. 115, 131, 168, 169, 170 (photographs: Novello Gamberini)

Maywald, Paris: pp. 108, 109, 139 (arrangements: Pierre Balmain)

Michel Nahmias, Paris: pp. 13, 16, 19 at the top, 22, 35, 41, 45, 55, 57, 71, 73, 75, 77, 91, 93, 95, 97, 99, 113, 119, 121, 129, 133, 141, 143, 153, 157, 159, 163, 173, 177, 179, 181, 203

National Association of Flower Arrangement Society of Great Britain: p. 83 (photograph and arrangement)

Schöner Wohnen, Hamburg: pp. 49, 50, 174 at the top, 175, 197, 198, 199, 201 (photographs and arrangements)

Jocelyn Steward, Norwich: p. 191 (photograph and arrangement)

Claude Voncken, Paris: pp. 12, 14, 15, 17, 18, 19 at the bottom, 20, 21, 25, 29, 33 (arrangement: Arène), 37; with the collaboration of Knoll International, Paris: 39, 52, 53; 61, 63, 65, 67, 69, 79, 87, 89, 105, 107, 127, 149 (arrangement: Arène), 151, 155, 160, 161, 167, 183

Tom Wier, New York: pp.51 (by kind permission of *House Beautiful,* New York), 192, 193, 194 (photographs and arrangements)

The arrangements, where the name of the flower decorator is not mentioned, are created by Jacques Bédat.

This book was printed in May 1969 by Imprimerie Paul Attinger S.A., Neuchâtel
Setting by Photo-composition Buri Druck, Bern
Photolithos by Atesa, Geneva
Binding by H. & J. Schumacher, Bern
Layout and design by André Rosselet, Auvernier
Drawings by Jean-Paul Chablais, Fribourg
Printed in Switzerland